# PRAIRIE JUSTICE

## The Hanging of Mike Hack

PATRONS OF THE SOCIETY

Professor Constance Backhouse
Chernos Flaherty Svonkin LLP
Gowling WLG
Hull & Hull LLP
Mr. Wayne Kerr
The Law Foundation of Ontario
McCarthy Tetrault
Osler, Hoskin & Harcourt LLP
Pape Chaudhury
Paliare Roland Rosenberg Rothstein LLP
The Hon. Robert Sharpe
Torys LLP
WeirFoulds LLP

The Osgoode Society is supported by a grant from The Law Foundation of Ontario.

The Society also thanks The Law Society of Upper Canada for its continuing support.

WAYNE SUMNER

# Prairie Justice

## The Hanging of Mike Hack

Published for the Osgoode Society for Canadian Legal History by
University of Toronto Press
Toronto Buffalo London

© Osgoode Society for Canadian Legal History
Toronto Buffalo London
utorontopress.com
Printed in the USA

ISBN 978-1-4875-6178-9 (cloth)
ISBN 978-1-4875-6180-2 (EPUB)
ISBN 978-1-4875-6179-6 (PDF)

___

**Library and Archives Canada Cataloguing in Publication**

Title: Prairie justice : the hanging of Mike Hack / Wayne Sumner.
Names: Sumner, L. W., author | Osgoode Society for Canadian Legal History, issuing body.
Description: Includes bibliographical references and index.
Identifiers: Canadiana (print) 20240427033 | Canadiana (ebook) 20240427114 | ISBN 9781487561789 (cloth) | ISBN 9781487561802 (EPUB) | ISBN 9781487561796 (PDF)
Subjects: LCSH: Hack, Mike, –1929 – Trials, litigation, etc. | LCSH: Murder – Saskatchewan – Case studies. | LCSH: Murder – Investigation – Saskatchewan – Case studies. | LCSH: Trials (Murder) – Saskatchewan – Case studies. | LCSH: Hanging – Saskatchewan – Case studies. | LCSH: Justice, Administration of – Saskatchewan – Case studies.
Classification: LCC HV6535.C32 S28 2024 | DDC 364.152/3097124 – dc23

___

Cover design: Val Cooke
Cover images: Mike Hack mug shots. Library and Archives Canada; iStock.com/tomograf; iStock.com/vitalssss

We wish to acknowledge the land on which the University of Toronto Press operates. This land is the traditional territory of the Wendat, the Anishnaabeg, the Haudenosaunee, the Métis, and the Mississaugas of the Credit First Nation.

University of Toronto Press acknowledges the financial support of the Government of Canada, the Canada Council for the Arts, and the Ontario Arts Council, an agency of the Government of Ontario, for its publishing activities.

 Canada Council for the Arts   Conseil des Arts du Canada

 ONTARIO ARTS COUNCIL
CONSEIL DES ARTS DE L'ONTARIO
an Ontario government agency
un organisme du gouvernement de l'Ontario

Funded by the Government of Canada   Financé par le gouvernement du Canada

*For my father*

# Contents

*Foreword* ix

*Preface* xi

1 Settlement   3

2 May 1928   12

3 How Justice Can Miscarry   29

4 October 1928   35

5 The Roads Not Taken   50

6 "He was German, he was deaf and a little simple"   69

7 The Royal Prerogative of Mercy   89

8 January 1929   108

9 The Bigger Picture   116

*Notes*   131

*Bibliography*   145

*Index*   151

# Foreword

*Prairie Justice: The Hanging of Mike Hack* is a deeply researched case study of a capital murder case from Saskatchewan in the 1920s. Although Mike Hack was deaf, and although his case was not famous, and it was not reported, its very ordinariness makes it a fascinating and instructive study of the criminal justice process in Canadian history from which we can learn a great deal about the "every day" operation of the criminal justice system. Hack's trial and conviction happened very quickly by current-day standards, and his appeal for executive clemency was cursorily rejected. Wayne Sumner takes us carefully through the crime, the police investigation, the arrest and trial, and then poses intriguing questions about whether, and why, we might label the case one of wrongful conviction.

The purpose of the Osgoode Society for Canadian Legal History is to encourage research and writing in the history of Canadian law. The Society, which was incorporated in 1979 and is registered as a charity, was founded at the initiative of the Honourable R. Roy McMurtry, and officials of the Law Society of Upper Canada. The Society seeks to stimulate the study of legal history in Canada by supporting researchers, collecting oral histories, and publishing volumes that contribute to legal-historical scholarship in Canada. This year's books bring the total published since 1981 to 125, in all fields of legal history – the courts, the judiciary, and the legal profession, as well as the history of crime and punishment, women and law, law and economy, the legal treatment of Indigenous peoples and ethnic minorities, and famous cases and significant trials in all areas of the law.

Current directors of the Osgoode Society for Canadian Legal History are Constance Backhouse, Heidi Bohaker, Brendan Brammall, Bevin Brookbank, Shantona Chaudhury, Paul Davis, Linda Silver Dranoff, Timothy Hill, Ian Hull, Mahmud Jamal, Waleed Malik, Rachel McMillan,

Dana Peebles, Linda Plumpton, David Rankin, Paul Schabas, Robert Sharpe, Jon Silver, Alex Smith, Lorne Sossin, Michael Tulloch, and John Wilkinson.

Robert J. Sharpe
President

Jim Phillips
Editor-in-Chief

# Preface

On the morning of Tuesday 8 May 1928, the body of George Edey was discovered buried in the manure pile on his farm, about three miles west of the village of Duff, in east-central Saskatchewan. On the following day, a local itinerant farm labourer named Mike Hack was charged with his murder. Mike Hack's trial lasted three days, from 3 October to 5 October 1928, at the end of which the jury took less than two hours to find him guilty. Because capital punishment was mandatory for murder convictions at the time, he was duly sentenced to death. After an application for clemency was denied, Mike Hack was hanged in the courtyard of the Regina Jail in the early morning of 18 January 1929. He was buried in an unmarked grave in Regina Cemetery. At the time of his death, Mike Hack was twenty-seven years old.

So much, so straightforward. Except that it is not. There is much more to this story than these simple facts convey. It is beyond reasonable doubt that Mike Hack killed George Edey. But it is far less clear that he should have been convicted of the murder, and that, having been convicted, he should have been hanged for having committed it.

In this book, I aim to not only tell the fuller story of the legal fate of Mike Hack but also draw some lessons from the case. Therefore, this is a case study in Canadian legal history. However, I lack the usual credentials for writing such a case study; I'm neither a lawyer nor a historian. My professional career was spent teaching and writing philosophy, and so, the reader might legitimately wonder: what is a philosopher doing writing about an obscure 1920s murder case in rural Saskatchewan? The answer to that question is complicated.

My interest in the case originated due to some family connections to it. My father was born in 1909 on a farm about five miles east of Duff, whose population has never much exceeded one hundred. Three years later, his parents sold the farm and moved the family into the village itself. The murder therefore occurred near his hometown. But he also had more personal connections to the crime, or at least to its aftermath. By virtue of that, so do I.

Once George Edey's body was discovered, a coroner's inquest was quickly convened at the scene of the crime by John W. Matthews, justice of the peace in the nearby town of Melville, to ascertain the cause of death. Following Mike Hack's arrest, that same John Matthews presided over the preliminary inquiry, held in the Duff community hall, which aimed to determine whether there was sufficient evidence to send the case to trial. Besides being a prominent local citizen, John Matthews was my great-grandfather (my father's mother's father). Frank Sumner, my grandfather (my father's father), was a member of that coroner's jury.

My father was nineteen at the time of the murder and no longer living at home. Instead, he was pursuing a teaching career elsewhere in the province, where he would meet my mother and then marry her in 1930. Later in that decade, my parents moved east to Toronto, which is where I was born. But my father retained a lifelong interest in that murder. In Toronto, he pursued a successful career in the insurance business, from managing the Toronto branch of a major New York life insurance company to running a general insurance firm of his own. When he retired in the 1970s, he took up amateur genealogy and history as hobbies. Based on the research he undertook, he wrote a book on the history of Duff and the surrounding region, which he self-published in 1980, on the occasion of the seventy-fifth anniversary of Saskatchewan's becoming a province.[1] I will have occasion to refer to this book in the following chapters. In 1982, my father also published a history of the settlement of the nearby Pheasant Hills area by the Primitive Methodist Colonization Company, on the centenary of the first arrival of the settlers to the region.[2]

In March 1982, my father received a letter from Rita Csada, a resident of Gravelbourg, Saskatchewan, whose husband Lyle was a grandson of Mike Hack's older sister Elizabeth. Ms. Csada reminded him of that 1928 murder and encouraged him to investigate it. By 1982, only one of Mike Hack's siblings was still living: his younger sister Dorothy (also known as Dora), who apparently believed that her brother might have been innocent of the crime. Now having some time on his hands, my father agreed to investigate it. In those pre-internet days, the relevant documents had to be either examined on site or requested by mail and then photocopied and sent by the same means. Using this method, over the course of a few months, he managed to compile a formidable amount of documentation concerning the crime, the police investigation, the preliminary inquiry, the subsequent trial, the application for clemency, and the execution. He also wrote to many people who were either alive when the crime was committed or who had been told of it by older generations of their families. The information he collected led him to doubt Dora's theory of Mike Hack's innocence, but he did nonetheless come to think that both the conviction and the denial of clemency were miscarriages of justice. His plan was to write a book substantiating those conclusions.

Unfortunately, my father died suddenly and unexpectedly in December 1982, before he could complete his work on the case. I inherited his research materials, with the vague intention of finishing his work someday. However, I had a career to manage and philosophy books to write, so I stored his papers in a box, to be returned to when the time was right. I rediscovered that box in 2019, when my wife and I were decluttering the basement of our house. Since I had also retired in 2008, I no longer had an excuse to not look into what he had managed to put together nearly forty years earlier. When I did, I became as fascinated by the case as he had been, even though I lacked the childhood connection to it. The result of that fascination is this book.

I realize that I cannot expect readers to be interested in this case just because I have family ties to it. There has to be more, and there is. But it isn't the extra that is commonly delivered by most "true crime" books. The murder was indeed brutal, but I will not be dwelling on the lurid details. The case is of wider interest for the light it sheds on some enduring themes in the history of Canadian criminal law: unfitness to stand trial, the defence of insanity, ineffective assistance of counsel, wrongful conviction, and miscarriage of justice. One other theme that has a prominent role in the story – the royal prerogative of mercy – also still officially exists, but its rationale was largely lost when the death penalty was abolished in 1976.

Some of the chapters to follow are purely narrative, as they trace the story through the murder investigation, the arrest of Mike Hack, the preliminary inquiry and trial, the application for clemency, and Mike Hack's execution. Other chapters, however, have a different purpose: to explore the aforementioned legal themes and explain their bearing on this case. These more analytical chapters are meant, among other things, to build an argument towards two conclusions: that Mike Hack's conviction for the murder of George Edey was wrongful, and hence a miscarriage of justice, and that the subsequent denial of clemency was a further miscarriage of justice. In other words, my father was right.

At various stages of the judicial process, there were key players who could have steered the narrative in a direction that would have spared Mike Hack's life. But none of them took the trouble to do so because none of them cared enough about the fate of this unremarkable child of German Lutheran immigrants, least of all his own defence counsel. The chapters that follow will, among other things, apportion responsibility for Mike Hack's fate among the appropriate parties. However, apart from these particularities of the case, there is also a larger lesson to be learned from the story about access to justice for the poor and marginalized.

Most, but not all, of the sources on which I have relied in researching this story are cited in standard scholarly fashion. In several places, I have quoted extensively from letters written to my father in 1982 by various people connected to Mike Hack, or to others who were on the scene when the events depicted in the narrative occurred. I have the originals of those letters in my possession.

More importantly, the records of the various stages of the judicial process, especially the trial, are stored in Library and Archives Canada: Department of Justice file RG13, Vol. 1549, File CC283, Mike Hack (Parts 1–3). I have all of these documents in electronic form and have cited them frequently, without continually reproducing this full reference. For enabling my access to these LAC records, I am grateful to Michel Brideau, consultation and reproduction clerk, Public Services Branch; Catherine Butler, archivist, Public Services Branch; and Alison Pier, Reference Services.

In my pursuit of other relevant documents, I have been fortunate to have had the able assistance of the following people: Amber Czechmeister, city clerk, Melville; Alan Kilpatrick, co-director and librarian, Legal Resources, Law Society of Saskatchewan; Donna Mucha, secretary, Melville Heritage Museum; David Nielsen, executive director, Access to Information and Privacy and Information Management, Privy Council Office; Amy Putnam, library assistant, University Archives and Special Collections, University of Saskatchewan; Teresa Redlick, reference archivist, Provincial Archives of Saskatchewan; Lloyd Schmidt, Melville Advance; and Bev Tourney, deputy local registrar, Court of King's Bench, Yorkton.

I have been directed to very valuable academic resources by some law and criminology colleagues who know the criminal justice system, and its history, far better than I do. Many thanks to Hamar Foster, Rosemary Gartner, Jim Phillips, and Kent Roach for enabling me to pursue the various issues raised by Mike Hack's involvement in that system, and for saving me from several embarrassing mistakes. I am also grateful to Kent McNeil, Karen Sumner, Kim Varma, and Heather Wright, all of whom read the manuscript, at various stages of development, and contributed many valuable suggestions for improvement. The comments and outright corrections provided by the two anonymous reviewers of the manuscript also led to many improvements. Tom Hurka suggested leads that steered the narrative in some unexpected and surprising new directions. For a quite different kind of assistance, I am grateful to Rita and Lyle Csada, my only remaining personal connections to the events of 1928. But I owe a particular debt of gratitude to Jim Phillips who, besides providing extensive comments on the manuscript, also encouraged the development of this unlikely project and facilitated its inclusion in the series published for the Osgoode Society for Canadian Legal History.

Finally, I owe my greatest debt to my father, whose interest in this case eventually ignited my own. This book is dedicated to his memory.

# PRAIRIE JUSTICE

## The Hanging of Mike Hack

# 1
# Settlement

Start east from Regina on the Trans-Canada Highway, and then about twenty kilometres outside the city, angle left at Balgonie onto Provincial Highway 10. Continue on this route through Fort Qu'Appelle and then Balcarres, until the highway starts to follow the railway. A few kilometres after crossing Highway 617, the road bends gently to the south to skirt a small settlement, before resuming its previous course. The road sign states the name of this settlement: Duff.

There isn't much to see there now, but in its heyday, Duff was a small yet bustling community. Since it owed its origin, and subsequent development, to the railway, it is fitting that it was named for a railwayman: A.E. Duff, the then chief passenger agent at Winnipeg for the Western Division of the Grand Trunk Pacific. The regional economy at the time was entirely agricultural. By the eve of the First World War, farming had been established in the area for three decades. This involved some livestock, poultry, and dairy, but mostly cereal grains: oats, barley, rye, and, above all, wheat. For a farm to be economically viable, only a small portion of a farmer's crop would be retained for food, and the rest had to find a market. Moving grain from field to final market destination required access to the railway, where rail cars could be loaded for transport east to the lakehead ports of Fort William and Port Arthur (now Thunder Bay). Grain shipment points along rail lines were spaced at intervals that enabled farmers situated farthest from the railway to deliver a load of grain by horse and wagon and return home in a single day. When the Grand Trunk Pacific branch line from Melville to Regina opened in August 1911, the site of Duff was an ideal location for this purpose. Situated about twenty kilometres southwest of the town of Melville, it could serve farmers for whom travelling to the larger municipality was impractical. Once the rail connection was in place, grain elevators were built in the community by three different companies – Security (1911), Atlas (1916), and Matheson-Lindsay (1923) – thus enabling the local farmers to sell their grain to the province, the country, and the world.

Buoyed by high grain prices through the war years, by 1920 Duff had achieved a population of 111, sufficient to officially graduate in status from hamlet to village. The site occupied twenty-two hectares in a long, roughly trapezoidal shape along the rail line. Its street network was anchored by Melville Road to the south and Railway Avenue to the north, where the grain elevators and railway station were situated beside the tracks. The side streets connecting these main roads reflected the triumphant monarchism of the age: Queen, King, Victoria, Edward, Alexandra, and George – all were represented. Along those streets, one could find all the amenities needed by the local farmers: a general store, where they could purchase seed and other supplies; a Massey Harris Equipment shop; a post office; a garage; a blacksmith; and a branch of the Merchants Bank of Canada. A one-room school opened in 1912, followed by a larger brick structure in 1921, with separate junior and senior rooms. Other markers of a vibrant village life included a barbershop and pool room, an ice cream parlour, a sports ground that could be converted to an ice rink in the winter, and an Orange Lodge that functioned as a community hall for multiple functions from town meetings to Saturday evening dances. The opportunity for worship on Sundays was provided by three churches (Anglican, Lutheran, and United).

Having peaked in 1920, world grain prices declined through the following decade, until they collapsed entirely after the stock market crash of 1929. Through the ensuing Dust Bowl of the 1930s, Saskatchewan farmers found their crops devastated by drought, plagues of grasshoppers, and hail. Net farming income for the province declined from $363 million in 1928 to $11 million in 1933, and by 1937, persistent crop failures had rendered two-thirds of the farm population destitute. Between 1931 and 1941 a quarter of a million people left the prairie provinces to head to British Columbia or Ontario. Most of these were from Saskatchewan, which had been hit the hardest. The Great Depression initiated the trend towards rural depopulation in the province, which eased somewhat after the Second World War but was never reversed.

Though the east-central area of the province around Melville fared better through the Dust Bowl years than many regions farther west and south, the population of Duff nonetheless fell from its peak of 122 in 1931 to 94 in 1941. It continued to decline after the war, though at a slower rate. For a while, the village did manage to retain its important role as the local railway shipping point for farmers to sell their grain. However, as horsepower gave way to mechanization, farmers became

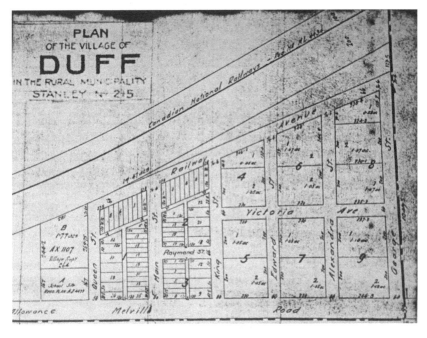

1.1. Duff town plan

Source: Len W. Sumner, *Raw Prairie to Grain Elevators*

able to transport larger loads of grain over longer distances, and the local wooden elevators gradually came to be replaced by larger, more centralized concrete facilities.

Duff's elevators are long gone now, along with the passenger station that once served the community (it now sits in the Melville Heritage Museum). Freight trains still run on the adjacent tracks, but they do not stop at Duff anymore. What remains on the site are a few scattered houses, open fields, and dirt roads with empty lots and abandoned vehicles. Based on the 2021 census, Duff's population had dwindled to just twenty-five residents living in nine of its sixteen private dwellings. Those who still live there work elsewhere, mostly in Melville. The school has vanished, and the churches are shuttered and crumbling. The only remaining public building on the site is the post office, serving an ever-dwindling clientele. On 1 January 2022, Duff lost the village status it had attained just over a century earlier. Having fallen below the prescribed minimum population for a village in two consecutive censuses, Duff was reconstituted as a Special Service Area within the Rural Municipality of Stanley No. 215.[1]

On the map, Duff stands as the apex of a narrow isosceles triangle whose base is defined by the towns of Lemberg and Neudorf, about eighteen kilometres to the south and about fourteen kilometres apart on Highway 22 and the Canadian Pacific Railway line. Both towns were founded in the 1890s by German immigrants and named for towns in Galicia – part of the Austro-Hungarian Empire at the time and now straddling the border between Poland and Ukraine (Lemberg is the German name for the city of Lviv, now located in western Ukraine). Within the perimeter of the triangle lies an area of gently rolling farmland dotted with sloughs (ponds or wetlands), drained by the two branches of the Pheasant Creek and dominated by the ridge of the Pheasant Hills on a southwest-to-northeast orientation. The landscape of the area confounds the naive visitor from the east, who expects Saskatchewan to be flat. Instead, like much of the rest of the province, its topography was formed by the movements of glaciers that carved the surface into mounds and depressions. Flat or not, there is no doubt about its suitability for farming. One of the earliest settlers, in the 1880s, reported that "the soil is rich and unsurpassed for grain growing."[2] So it proved to be.

The province of Saskatchewan divides into two broad sections: the Canadian shield to the north, characterized by coniferous forests, rugged rock exposures, and many lakes, and the prairie ecozone to the south, with its arable farmland. Where the prairie meets the shield lies a well-treed parkland belt. The Pheasant Hills area, which intersperses parkland and grassland, is situated between the Qu'Appelle valley to the south and the Beaver Hills to the north. The area lies in the black soil zone of the province, where the surface layer is characterized by high levels of organic matter, ideal for planting crops.

For at least a millennium before the arrival of the first Europeans, the prairies were the exclusive domain of various Indigenous peoples, their distribution shifting over time.[3] By the latter half of the nineteenth century, what were then the Districts of Saskatchewan, Assiniboia, and Athabaska were populated mainly by the Plains Cree, with small pockets of Assiniboia, Saulteaux, and Sioux. After Confederation, the new government of Canada quickly adopted a policy of attracting immigrants, chiefly from Europe and the United States, to settle and develop the western plains. However, the government was bound by the Royal Proclamation of 1763 to recognize that these lands were already occupied by First Nations. The right to settle immigrants on them could be acquired only by negotiating treaties between the Crown and the resident Indigenous peoples. Beginning in the early 1870s, a series of such treaties effectively reduced these First Nations territories to a patchwork of fairly small reserves. This process commenced with Treaty 2 in 1871, which dealt mainly with Manitoba but extended into (what would become) southeastern Saskatchewan. Treaty 4 in 1874 then established numerous Plains Cree and Saulteaux reserves in southern and east-central Saskatchewan. By the 1880s, these reserves were interspersed with the farm plots that were being allocated to the newly arriving immigrants. In the Pheasant Hills area, for example, the Okanese Reserve No. 82 was located about three miles due west of Duff, on the northern boundary of George Edey's farm.

To oversee and manage the process of settling Western Canada, the federal government passed the *Dominion Lands Act* on 14 April 1872, modeled on similar legislation passed ten years earlier in the United States.[4] Under the terms of this act, for a registration fee of $10, prospective settlers would be granted a homestead, which they could occupy and farm. Implementing this massive allocation scheme required devising a system for identifying homestead sites. The solution was to define a grid, using both north–south and east–west reference points. For the former, the meridians of longitude were the natural choice. The Dominion Land Survey (DLS), which began in 1871, employed seven of these longitudinal markers, numbering westward from (what it defined as) the prime meridian, located just west of Winnipeg.[5] The reference point for the eastern half of Saskatchewan was the second meridian, which later came to define the northern part of the border between Saskatchewan and Manitoba. Range boundaries were then marked at six-mile intervals numbering westward from this meridian. These ranges defined the columns on the grid. (All distances from this point will be given in miles, since surveyors at the time used imperial measures.)

For an east–west baseline, the DLS adopted the 49th parallel of latitude – the border with the United States. Township lines were likewise marked in six-mile intervals numbering north from the US border. These townships formed the rows on the grid. This grid system also defined the principal road network, with (mostly unpaved) roads at six-mile intervals – range roads running north–south and township roads running east–west – unless interrupted by natural obstacles, such as hills, creeks, or sloughs. In the 1920s, before Provincial Highway 10 was built, the road from Regina to Melville did not follow its current diagonal southwest-to-northeast route. Instead, it ran alternately east and north along the township and range roads, until it reached its destination. One of its township legs ran along the southern boundary of

1.2. Pheasant Hills

Source: Len W. Sumner, *Raw Prairie to Grain Elevators*

Duff. The DLS also designated township road allowances at one-mile intervals and range road allowances two miles apart, although roads were not actually built on all of these allowances.

So, we have columns (ranges) and rows (townships) whose intersections define six-mile squares, each identified by its range and township number. These squares were then subdivided into thirty-six sections, each one mile square (640 acres). Perhaps not exactly square: because the lines of meridian converge at the north pole, both townships and sections were slightly narrower on their northern boundary. Sections within a township were numbered along the rows, starting on the southernmost row and then progressing northward. The numbering was alternately east-to-west and west-to-east. Sections were in turn subdivided into quarters, each a half-mile square, identified by their compass-point orientation within the section: NE, NW, SE, or SW. A homestead allotment was typically one of these quarter-sections (160 acres), whose full identification (its address, as it were) was given by its orientation, section number, township number, and range number

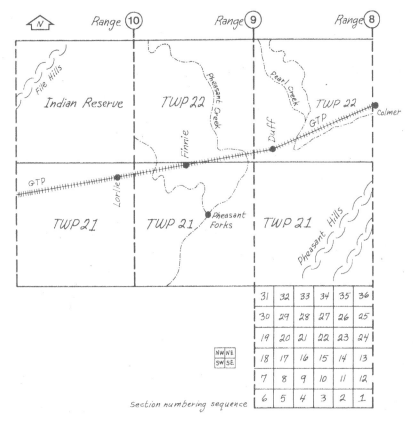

1.3. Pheasant Hills survey grid
Source: Len W. Sumner, *Raw Prairie to Grain Elevators*

relative to the second meridian. Therefore, the site NE-14-20-9-W2 was the northeast quarter of section 14 in township 20 and range 9 west of the second meridian. Confusing? This diagram for the Pheasant Hills area should make it a little clearer.

Homesteaders did not immediately acquire ownership of their assigned quarter-section site. The conditions to be satisfied to gain patent – or title – to the site varied over time. Under the original 1872 act, the settler needed to cultivate and reside on the land for three years. In subsequent years, these conditions became much more specific and exacting. By 1886, for example, the settler was required to commence cultivation of the site within six months of occupancy, break and prepare for crop at least five acres in the first year and at least ten additional acres in the second year, build a habitable house before the end of the second year, and commence residence on the homestead by the beginning of the third year.

These were not easy conditions to meet. The immigrant family would need to find some place to live until they were able to move onto the homestead itself. The work of clearing, tilling, and planting five (or ten) acres of prairie grassland required equipment – at the minimum horses and a plough. Since water was a necessity, a well would need to be drilled. Building a house (and a barn) required not only labour but also tools and building materials. Since trees were not plentiful on much of the grassland prairie, many homesteaders' first habitation on their site was a sod house. All these tasks were to be carried out in an environment that was often harsh, especially over the winter months. It is not surprising that the failure rate was high: by one estimate, 40 per cent of homesteaders never managed to acquire patent on their site.[6] Those who did succeed would gain the option of purchasing an adjoining quarter-section, which they would then also have to improve.

Notwithstanding the obstacles faced by the early settlers, by the 1920s, all of the arable land in the Pheasant Hills region – basically, everything that was not wetland, woodland, or ridgeland – was divided into quarter- or half-section family farms. Buoyed by waves of immigrants from Europe and the United States, the population of Saskatchewan grew from less than 20,000 in 1880 to just under half a million in 1911. By the start of the First World War, most of the grassland and parkland areas of the province had been settled by members of diverse ethno-religious groups who had formed their own enclaves. Ethnic "bloc settlements" of this kind were common throughout the province.[7] Many of the settlers attracted to the Pheasant Hills area were British, including a large number brought over from England by the Primitive Methodist Colonization Company, who tended to take up homesteads in the northern part of the area, near Duff. As early as 1883, the Company had established over a hundred homesteaders at the settlement of Pheasant Forks.[8] Bypassed by the railways, the settlement was later abandoned, but the settlers remained.

Despite the fact that the province was on record as wishing to preserve Saskatchewan "for English-speaking peoples,"[9] there was also a sizeable influx of ethnic groups from other parts of Europe: Swedes, Norwegians, Icelanders, Hungarians, Romanians, among others. The southern part of the Pheasant Hills area attracted a significant number of ethnic Germans, both Protestant and Catholic, forming one of the largest German colonies in the province.[10] The German influence in the area can be seen to this day in some of its place names, especially Lemberg and Neudorf, as well as in the plentiful number of German surnames in rosters of the homesteaders. Based on the 2021 census, residents of German origin are still the largest ethnic group in Saskatchewan. By contrast with Duff, both Lemberg and Neudorf remain thriving towns to this day, with a 2021 population of about 250 each.

Among those early German Lutheran settlers were Mathias Hack and his wife Dorothea. (In some documents the family surname is spelled "Haack," but I will stick to the more common spelling.) Mathias was born in October 1854 in Gassendorf, Galicia, while Dorothea Ulmer was born in the same town nine years later. The couple married there in 1881. While still in their homeland, Mathias was employed as a carpenter, and he and Dorothea had three sons, only one of whom survived long enough to emigrate to Canada with his parents in 1888. Although serfdom had been abolished in the Austro-Hungarian Empire in 1848, many Galician peasants faced crippling debt, shrinking land holdings, and even the loss of their small plots, forcing entire families to labour once again on the landlord's estate. The average peasant farm was 2.5 hectares (about six acres), making Canada's promise of 160 acres of "free land" seem like paradise.

Having arrived in Canada, by September 1889, Mathias had turned to farming and was registered on a quarter-section homestead in southwestern Alberta. There, three more children followed, two boys and a girl. In 1894 the family moved east into Saskatchewan, where they occupied a quarter-section of land about three miles east of Lemberg on the road to Neudorf (for the record, NE-14–20–9-W2, the site used earlier for illustration). They acquired title to this site eight years later, in July 1902. Six more children were born there between 1895 and 1908, one of whom died at birth. Only one of the surviving children was a boy, who arrived on 16 March 1901. They named him Michael, but everyone called him Mike.

# 2
# May 1928

William Bannerman, the officer in charge of the Melville detachment of the Saskatchewan Provincial Police (SPP), was sitting at his desk on the evening of Monday 7 May 1928. He may have been thinking about his future. At the end of the month, the SPP was due to be disbanded, and Constable Bannerman would be out of a job.

Before Saskatchewan became a province in 1905, policing the district was the responsibility of the Royal Northwest Mounted Police, later the Royal Canadian Mounted Police (RCMP). In 1905, the new provincial government contracted with the RCMP to continue its policing duties. However, five years later the province saw fit to create the SPP, largely for the purpose of enforcing the provincial hotel and liquor regulations, which the federal authorities had refused to do. In 1916, during the war, the head of the RCMP volunteered the services of the organization as a cavalry unit in the Canadian Expeditionary Force. Since both the strength and the sphere of action of the SPP had gradually increased over the following years, it was ready to take over all the policing of Saskatchewan effective 1 January 1917. For the next decade or so, much of its energy was devoted to preventing the smuggling of liquor across the American border (in either direction) and to containing collateral activities such as the robbing of banks, post offices, and trains.

During this period, the RCMP had continued to maintain itself as a fairly powerful force within the province. It had a training centre in Regina, and it remained responsible for enforcing federal statutes such as the *Opium and Narcotic Drugs Act*. Primarily because it became uneconomical to maintain two parallel police forces, it was decided to revert to the prior arrangement whereby policing of the province would be the responsibility of the dominion force. Consequently, the SPP was to be disbanded on 31 May.[1] Constable Bannerman would not be transitioning to the new force; instead Constable James Watts of the

2.1. Edey's farm

Source: Saskatchewan Archives

Esterhazy SPP detachment would be transferring to the RCMP and replacing Bannerman in Melville.

But before exploring other career options, Constable Bannerman would find himself in the middle of a murder investigation.[2] The call that led to his involvement came in at 7:00 p.m. that Monday 7 May, from Tom Matthews, co-proprietor of the general store in Duff. Matthews wanted to report that a local farmer named George Edey had been missing since Tuesday 1 May, six days earlier.

Edey farmed a half-section of land about three miles west of Duff, extending south from the township road.[3] Born in England in 1885, Edey had immigrated to Canada in 1906 and had been farming in the area since 1914. Edey was unmarried, lived alone, and had no relatives in Canada; he was known locally as "a quiet, reserved man who made few social contacts."[4] Like most other farmers in the region, he grew wheat and oats, which he either kept for his own use or transported to Duff for sale to one of the grain agents. However, unlike most of his neighbours, he did not own the land he worked; instead, he leased it from a local man named Luke Battersby, who had been one of the original settlers in the area, arriving in 1882. Edey owned no mechanized farm equipment, which at that time was still relatively rare in the area. All the necessary work of ploughing, reaping, binding, mowing, and threshing was done either by hand or with the aid of Edey's seven horses, in whom he took great pride. Edey was renowned in the area for the exceptional care he took of those horses.

Reginald Ward, his neighbour to the south and east, was accustomed to seeing Edey working in his fields nearly every day. Around 6:00 p.m. on that Tuesday 1 May, Ward saw him unhitching his horses as usual. No one had seen him, or his horses, since.

Harry Bateman, the other co-proprietor of the general store, had been out to the farm on 6 May to check on Edey's whereabouts. He found

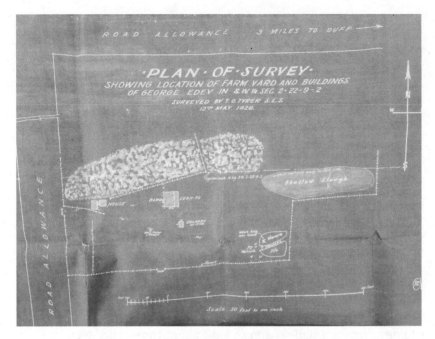

2.2. Survey of Edey's farm

Source: Saskatchewan Archives

the door of the farmhouse unlocked and signs that Edey had made a hurried departure. Dishes were spread all over the table, bedclothes were disarranged, and Edey's pipe was lying on the chair beside the bed. Bateman found the barn empty and three of Edey's horses running loose in the pasture.

On 7 May, Matthews asked Constable Bannerman to come to Duff to investigate the disappearance. Later that day, around 9:00 p.m. or 10:00 p.m., Matthews rang again to report that a local man named Mike Hack had been seen that evening, about five miles south of Duff, driving a team and wagon that belonged to the missing man. The person who had encountered Hack on the road was a local well-driller named Arthur Johnson. He had learned of Edey's disappearance two days earlier (5 May), and on the following day (6 May), he had driven to Edey's farm to determine whether he was truly missing. Once there, Johnson found the door of the house unlocked, all the horses missing from the barn, and no sign of Edey. On the evening of 7 May, Johnson was driving south of Duff, asking local farmers if they had seen anyone with four horses and a wagon. As he was returning to Duff, his car stalled and Hack approached from the north, driving the team and wagon. Hack told Johnson that he was heading to Neudorf. Johnson then drove back to Duff and informed Matthews, who in turn informed Constable Bannerman. At that point, Johnson and Bateman drove out to Edey's farm again but found no one there.

On the morning of Tuesday 8 May, Constable Bannerman drove from Melville to Duff to interview Matthews. He then decided to drive to Neudorf, accompanied by Johnson, to speak to members of Hack's family, including his mother and siblings. On the road just east of the village, the two men overtook Hack driving a team and wagon heading east towards the town of Dubuc. Johnson recognized the horses and wagon as belonging to Edey.

Upon being questioned by Constable Bannerman, Hack said that he had purchased seven horses from Edey for $700, in addition to horse collars, harnesses, and the wagon for $151. He had taken four of the horses and the wagon away from Edey's farm on 30 April. He produced two receipts dated 26 April, one for each purchase. He also said that he had helped Edey move from his farm to the village of Lorlie, some six miles to the west, where he was now staying.

At this point, four other local residents joined Constable Bannerman and Johnson. Louie Schick, Pete Gross, and Herman Kaduhr happened by in a car driven by Schick, and Fred Haverstock, a resident of Neudorf, arrived on the scene separately. All four, plus Johnson, witnessed Constable Bannerman's further questioning of Hack, with both questions and answers given in writing, since Hack was completely deaf. Schick wrote some of Constable Bannerman's questions in German, for Hack's benefit, and Kaduhr also assisted by interpreting answers that Hack wrote in German. Constable Bannerman questioned Hack about the receipts and asked him for a sample of his handwriting to compare with the handwriting on the receipts. Having compared the two, he concluded that the receipts had been forged.

Constable Bannerman asked Hack to put up the wagon and horses at a livery stable in Neudorf and to accompany him and Johnson to Lorlie to locate Edey. Passing Edey's farm on the way, Constable Bannerman decided to stop in to see if he had returned. He found both the house and the barn empty, but then noticed some loose dirt near the manure pile, which was located at some distance from the barn. When he went over to investigate, he stepped on something that gave a gurgling sound. Suspecting that there might be a body under the pile, Constable Bannerman asked Johnson to fetch a fork, which he used to remove some of the manure and straw. He uncovered the face of a dead man and asked Johnson whether he recognized who it was. George Edey was lying on his back covered by some eight or ten inches of manure and straw with both hands clasped over his chest. He was fully dressed with the exception of his cap, which was afterwards found beside the manure pile.

Constable Bannerman was now joined at the scene by Constable Watts of the SPP Esterhazy detachment, and by Luke Battersby, the owner of the farm that Edey rented. Battersby had contacted Constable Watts on the evening of 7 May concerning the disappearance of Edey. So, Constable Watts, along with Battersby, had come to the farm to investigate. Once at the scene, Constables Watts and Bannerman again interrogated Hack, with both questions and answers once more written. Hack told the officers that he had stayed overnight with George Edey on a few occasions, most recently on 29–30 April. He claimed to have last seen Edey when he left the farm at 8:00 a.m. on 30 April. He also claimed to have spent the next five nights at the farm near Dubuc (about 25 miles east of Neudorf) owned by his sister Dora and her husband George Hepting. Hack said that he spent the nights of 6 and 7 May at his mother's place in Neudorf.

Constable Watts then suspended the questioning to inform Hack of the charge on which he was being held and gave him the following warning in writing:

> Having learned the charge on which you are being arrested, you are not bound to say anything, but you must clearly understand that what you have to say will be taken down in writing and used as evidence against you at your trial. You have nothing to hope from any promise or favour or any threat which may have been held out to you to induce you to make any admission of your guilt, but whatever you say hereafter will be taken down in writing and used as evidence against you at your trial, notwithstanding such promise or threat.[5]

Having ascertained that Hack understood his rights, Constable Watts questioned him concerning Edey's horses that were currently in his possession. Hack again stated that he had purchased four horses from Edey on 26 April and took them with him when he left Edey's farm on 30 April. He also said that Edey had been feeling unwell and that he had intended to sell his farm and move to Lorlie. Constable Watts then showed Hack the two receipts and asked him who had made them out. When Hack said that Edey had done so, Constable Watts then asked him to write out the same information that was on the receipts. When Hack did so, the results resembled the handwriting on the receipts, including misspelling "hundred" as "hundret" and "Edey" as "Adey."

2.3. John Matthews
Source: Melville *Advance*

Immediately upon discovering Edey's body, Constable Bannerman notified John Matthews, father of Tom Matthews, who, besides being justice of the peace, was also the coroner for Melville. In Saskatchewan, as in the other provinces, the coroner played an important role in the initial investigation of suspicious deaths. Under the terms of the *Coroners Act*, he was obliged to inquire into any deaths in the locality "where there is reason to believe that the deceased died as the result of an accident under such circumstances as to require investigation."[6] Upon arriving in Duff, Matthews quickly determined that there was indeed such reason in Edey's case and instructed Bannerman to empanel a coroner's jury, whose six members were brought to Edey's farm to view the body before it was removed for postmortem examination. Constable Watts then attended the autopsy on Edey's body, which was performed at the farm by Dr. C.A. Findlay of the nearby town of Lemberg. An examination of Edey's head showed bruises under the scalp, hemorrhage, and a fracture of the inner table of the skull. Dr. Findlay removed the stomach and intestines of the deceased, which Constable Watts then handed over to J. Grant Lewis, the provincial analyst, for examination. Lewis worked under the direction of Dr. Frances McGill, the provincial pathologist, one of the first women to be employed in this role in Canada.[7] Later, on 12 May, Constable Watts received a report from Lewis: "I have made toxicologic examination of the stomach of George Edey, deceased ... I find no evidence of the presence of any poison."

At the coroner's inquest, held in the Orange Hall in Duff on the evening of 8 May and presided over by Matthews, Dr. Findlay testified as to cause of death:

> I found a cross-shaped laceration over the right parietal bone. A crescent shape laceration about one inch long over the right temple and a laceration one inch long on the left side of the occipital bone. There was extensive subcutaneous hemorrhage about the areas of these lacerations. There was also a laceration of the right ear, bruises on the left side of the neck and also one behind the right ear. There was a fracture of the inner table of the right parietal bone beneath the cross-shape laceration mentioned above. There was extensive subdural hemorrhage and the immediate cause of death was compression from this hemorrhage caused by the above injuries. The lacerations were evidently caused by a blunt instrument. I am quite satisfied the injuries were not self-inflicted. He had evidently been dead for several days. There must have been at least six blows struck to cause the injuries. There was no evidence of a bullet wound.[8]

Constable Bannerman then related the events leading up to his discovery of Edey's body and gave his opinion that the receipts that Hack had proffered were forgeries. Other witnesses testified to what they had observed in the days around the time of Edey's death. Ward confirmed that he had last seen Edey unhitching his horses on the evening of Tuesday 1 May. He further stated that the deceased visited him three days prior to that, when he appeared to be in the best of health, mentioned nothing about moving, and spoke as though he intended to work his land as usual. Ward also testified that in the early morning of

Wednesday 2 May, he saw Edey's horses and wagon being driven by his place, with one team hitched to the wagon and one team being led behind. He could not identify the driver, but he supposed that it must be Edey. Louie Gottinger, who owned the garage in Duff, testified that Hack came to his shop on 28 April carrying a gun and said that he had been to Edey's place to look at his car. Edmund Sutton and Harry Addis, who lived north and west of Edey's farm, gave testimony that Hack came to their place on 1 May and was carrying a rifle.

After consideration, the coroner's jury found that George Edey "came to his death on or about May 2nd 1928 ... by being struck on the head with a dull instrument by some person or persons unknown." Based on the evidence submitted at the inquest, the jury also recommended that Hack be held in police custody for investigation. Matthews then issued a warrant apprehending the accused, which Constable Bannerman duly executed. On the morning of 9 May, Constable Bannerman laid an Information and Complaint before Matthews, that "Mike Hack, of Neudorf, on or about the 2nd day of May 1928, at Sec. 2–22–9 W.2nd. Mer. in the province of Saskatchewan, did murder one George Edey, contrary to the C. C. of C."[9] Hack subsequently appeared before Matthews and was remanded in custody to the Regina Jail, to be held there pending a preliminary inquiry scheduled to begin on 16 May. However, at 11 a.m. on that date, he was brought to appear in Regina before W.B. Scott, Provincial Police Magistrate, where, on behalf of the prosecution, a request was made for a further remand in custody until 21 May. Once the request was granted, Hack was escorted back to the Regina Jail to await his preliminary inquiry on that date. Meanwhile, on the evening of Thursday 10 May, George Edey was buried in the cemetery at Pheasant Forks.

This was not the most complex or difficult criminal investigation that Constables Bannerman and Watts would ever conduct. Within a day of being notified of George Edey's disappearance, they had apprehended a suspect, and within two days, they had formally charged him with Edey's murder. The investigation had benefited immediately from two strokes of good fortune. Bannerman was quickly able to locate Hack, who was in possession of Edey's horses and wagon, with only an evidently dubious explanation of how he had acquired them. Then he literally stumbled over the body of the deceased during a chance stop at Edey's farm. Once cause of death had been established, a charge of murder against Hack was inevitable. All that remained, in the days following the charge, was to gather further pertinent evidence.

On Thursday 10 May, Corporal J.G. Metcalfe of the RCMP Melville detachment and Detective Sergeant Charles Dunnett of the Regina SPP

2.4. Mike Hack's mug shots
Source: Library and Archives Canada

detachment augmented the investigating team. On the previous day, Constable Watts had interviewed Dorothea Hack (Hack's mother), Dora Hepting (his sister), and George Hepting (his brother-in-law). During his interview with Dorothea, William Stanley Elliott, a barrister from Neudorf, arrived at the house and indicated that he would not allow her to make a statement. Elliott had previously acted for the Hack family in the matter of Mathias's estate, upon his death in 1925. Evidently, Elliot had been alerted by the family about Hack's detention by the police. Constable Watts explained that he was conducting a criminal investigation and that Dorothea was not the accused. Whereas Elliott had the right to protect his client, he could not interfere with Crown witnesses. Dorothea's statement was duly taken.

Dorothea said that Hack had turned up at her place around noon on Wednesday 2 May, with four horses that he said he had purchased from an Englishman, as well as a wagon, collars, and harnesses. After staying overnight, he then went away on Thursday morning, until he returned on Sunday 6 May. Dora and George Hepting confirmed that

2.5. Mick Hack's fingerprints

Source: Library and Archives Canada

Hack had stayed with them at their farm two and a half miles northwest of Dubuc, but said that he arrived with the horses and wagon and other equipment around 9:00 p.m. or 10:00 p.m. on Wednesday 2 May. (The statements by Hack's mother and by his sister and brother-in-law are therefore contradictory on this point: each claims that Hack stayed with them on the night of 2 May. I have chosen to accept the latter statement as the more reliable.) The Heptings also said that Hack had told them that the man who sold him the horses gave him a fur coat and rubber boots for helping him move from the farm.

Over the next few days, the officers involved in the investigation interviewed, and obtained statements from, a number of other local residents, including George Edey's neighbours. The information thus obtained enabled them to piece together a reasonably complete timeline of salient events over the two-week period leading up to Hack's apprehension on 8 May.

**24–30 April.** Hack was seen by many moving about in the area in which Edey lived. During this period, he stayed overnight on various people's farms, including those of William Diment, Bernard Enns, and Andrew Middleton. Diment's quarter-section lay about two miles southeast of Edey's half-section, while Middleton's half-section abutted Edey's on the east. Hack was observed to have a rifle in his possession. He told various people, including his brothers Fred and Matt, that he had purchased four horses from a farmer around Duff.

**Tuesday 1 May.** At about 9:00 a.m., Edmund Sutton saw Hack coming from Edey's property, carrying a rifle. In the afternoon, Middleton also saw Hack in the vicinity of Edey's farm. At various times during this day Edey was seen plowing his field by four of his near neighbours: Sutton, Middleton, Ward, and Louis Lutz. Lutz's farm lay due south of Edey's, separated from it by the railway line and the quarter-section owned by the Ulmer family. On the same day, Hack stopped in at Sutton's place and inquired about one of Edey's horses. Around 9:00 p.m., Sutton saw a man he could not identify approach Edey's farm from the direction of Duff.

**Wednesday 2 May.** Various neighbours began to notice unusual circumstances on Edey's farm. The man himself was nowhere to be seen, four of his horses and wagon were missing, and three other horses were running loose in the field. At around 6:00 a.m. that day, Ward saw four horses and a wagon being driven east past his place by someone he could not identify, a sighting that was confirmed by May Ward, his wife. Matt Lutz, whose half-section lay directly east of Ward's, reported the same sighting at 6:45 a.m.: two horses hitched to the wagon and two tied behind. He watched the wagon and horses proceed east and then turn south. At 8:00 a.m. or 9:00 a.m., Fred Gottinger saw a man with a wagon and four horses approaching from the west and then turning south. Around 9:00 a.m., Willie Ulmer saw Hack drive past his school with four horses. At 10:30 a.m., Willie's brother Sam saw a man with four horses and a wagon heading south on the road from Duff to Neudorf. Around 11:30 a.m., Joseph Mann encountered Hack driving the wagon eastbound about a mile west of Neudorf (about ten miles south of Edey's farm). Hack arrived at his mother's place in Neudorf around noon. Mann then saw him again between 1:00 p.m. and 2:00 p.m. on the road east of Neudorf, heading east towards Dubuc. As previously established, Hack arrived at the Hepting farm around that evening with the four horses and the wagon and stayed the night.

**3–5 May.** Hack continued to stay with his sister and brother-in-law in Dubuc.

**Thursday 3 May.** Andrew Middleton came by Edey's farm at around 6:00 p.m. to deliver a plug of tobacco he had purchased for Edey in Duff. He found no one at home, no horses in the stable, and Edey's wagon missing. At around 7:00 p.m., Edmund Sutton came to Edey's farm, found no one at home and no horses or harness in the stable, and saw the plug of tobacco on the doorknob where Middleton had left it.

**Friday 4 May.** Louis Lutz and Reginald Ward came by Edey's farm at around 8:00 p.m. They found no one at home and no horses or harness in the stable.

**Saturday 5 May.** Hack left the Hepting farm at 10:00 a.m. with one team and the wagon, saying that he planned to go to Neudorf and then north to Edey's farm to pick up more equipment. Hack arrived at his mother's place in Neudorf about 6:00 p.m. and stayed the night.

**Sunday 6 May.** Bateman visited Edey's farm to check on him. He found the farmhouse unlocked and the barn empty. He also saw signs of a hurried departure – dishes and bedclothes in disarray. On the same day, Johnson also drove to Edey's farm – separately – and found the door unlocked and the barn empty.

**Monday 7 May.** Hack came by Phillip Armbruster's farm (five miles west of Neudorf) with the wagon and two horses and asked him to clip the horses' manes. At about 8:00 p.m., Johnson encountered Hack, with the horses and wagon, heading south on the road about five miles south of Duff. Hack again stayed the night at his mother's place.

**Tuesday 8 May.** Hack was found by Constable Bannerman and Johnson with the horses and wagon, and some of George Edey's personal effects, heading east on the highway between Neudorf and Dubuc.

The information that the investigating officers gathered from these various sources enabled them to put together a theory about how, when, and why the crime occurred:

In January 1928, Mike Hack bought a half-section of land adjoining Dora and George Hepting's farm near Dubuc but, lacking both horses and equipment, had no means to farm it. George Edey had a reputation in the area for having the finest horses, so Hack decided that he must have Edey's horses. He had no money to purchase them, so decided that he would acquire them by another means. He was seen walking west from Duff along the railway track on the evening of Tuesday 1 May. He was the man that Edmund Sutton saw approaching Edey's farm around 9:00 p.m. that evening. Once at the farm, Hack asked to stay overnight and was allowed to sleep in the hayloft of Edey's barn. Sometime around midnight, Edey went to the barn, as was his custom, to feed his horses. When he climbed the ladder to the loft to pitch hay down to the mangers, Hack struck him on the head with the butt of his rifle, and continued hitting him until Edey was dead. Hack dragged the body from the barn to the manure pile and buried it under some straw. He then hitched two of Edey's horses to the wagon, tied two others behind, and turned the three other horses out into the field. He took with him some additional collars and harnesses, plus a coat and pair of rubber boots belonging to Edey, and set out on the road, first south to Neudorf and then east to the farm of his sister Dora and George Hepting near Dubuc. Sometime thereafter, while staying at his mother's place, Hack used her receipt book to forge receipts for the horses, wagon, collars, and harnesses, dating them to 26 April.

Motive, means, and opportunity. This was the theory the prosecution would eventually put to the jury in Hack's murder trial, and it is the theory that the jury would accept. But before that stage, a prior step was necessary.

The process of determining whether a person suspected of a crime should stand trial changed in various ways in the nineteenth century, until what had become the "preliminary inquiry" was detailed at length in the 1892 *Criminal Code*.[10] The principal function of the preliminary inquiry has been to serve as a procedural safeguard in the prosecution of the more serious offences by providing a pre-trial hearing before a magistrate, whose task is to determine whether there is sufficient evidence to put the accused to the jeopardy of a criminal trial.[11] In English law, this function was once also served by the institution of the grand jury, a practice which survived Confederation in Canada but by the 1920s had been discarded in favour of the alternative procedure. The burden of the Crown prosecutor at the preliminary inquiry is to present the witnesses on which they will rely at the trial. Defence counsel is entitled to cross-examine them as well as to call their own witnesses. The hearing is open to the public, but often, the press are not able to report the evidence heard (though in the case of Hack, they were able to do so). Besides its function of testing the prosecution's evidence and weeding out cases that are not strong enough to justify the time and expense of a trial, the preliminary inquiry has also served a secondary "discovery" purpose of providing the defence with prior notice of the evidence that the Crown plans to adduce at trial.

In 1928, a preliminary inquiry was automatic in the case of an indictable offence such as murder. More recently, however, the procedure has become much less common.[12] As a result of amendments to the *Criminal Code* in 2004, a hearing will now be held only upon the request of one of the parties (almost always the accused, but the Crown may make such a request as well). In the absence of such a request, the accused will simply be committed to stand trial on a date fixed by the court. This change was prompted in part by the growing length of cross-examinations in preliminary inquiries, which had the effect of significantly delaying the trial of the accused. This consideration became even more urgent following the 2016 Supreme Court decision that placed strict limits on time elapsed between charge and trial.[13] Furthermore, by 2004, the preliminary inquiry had already lost much of its crucial "discovery" role, as a result of the Court's earlier 1991 ruling that the Crown has a legal duty to disclose all relevant information to the defence.[14] The Court later acknowledged that "the incidental function of the preliminary inquiry as a discovery mechanism has lost much of its relevance."[15]

The Orange Hall at Duff was packed for the preliminary inquiry in the case of Hack, which convened at 2:30 p.m. on Monday 21 May. Many other local residents were unable to gain entrance, and many women were reported to be among those present.[16] Like the coroner's inquest, the proceeding was conducted by John Matthews. The Crown's burden of presenting the evidence against Hack was discharged by Ernest Walter Gerrand, King's Counsel (KC), a prominent lawyer based in Melville, who had been educated at the University of Manitoba. Seven years later, Gerrand would win a by-election to the Saskatchewan Legislative Assembly, where he served a three-year term as a Liberal. The request that he conduct the prosecution had been made by T.C. Goldsmith, the Inspector commanding the Regina Division of the SPP, on the ground that Gerrand was the agent of the attorney general for the Judicial District of Melville.

Hack was represented at the inquiry by the aforementioned William Elliott of Neudorf, but also by Percival McCuaig Anderson, KC, of the Regina law firm of Anderson, Bayne, and Company. Percy Anderson was a successful and experienced lawyer who had graduated from Queen's University with an Honours B.A. in Political Science and

2.6. Percy Anderson
Source: Saskatchewan Archives

History and had been admitted to the bar in Manitoba, having been apprenticed to a Winnipeg law firm. In 1909, he relocated to Saskatchewan and, in 1919, received the designation of King's Counsel. Over the course of his career, he appeared in over two hundred recorded cases at the trial level of the Court of King's Bench, at the Saskatchewan Court of Appeal, and at least twice at the Privy Council. While most of these cases were civil, a dozen or so were criminal, most of them being argued on appeal. Later, during the 1930s, he was twice elected to the Legislative Assembly as a Liberal, before being appointed to the Court of King's Bench in 1938 and, later in 1946, to the Saskatchewan Court of Appeal.

Since Hack was completely deaf, he was shown the Information and Complaint laid against him in writing before it was read out in court. Anderson requested that Hack's deafness be noted in the minutes but waived the submission of oral testimony to him in writing. He proposed that the inquiry proceed as though Hack was able to hear, saying that he would summarize the evidence for him afterward. On the first day of the hearing, Gerrand presented nine witnesses, including Dr. C.A. Findlay, who had conducted the autopsy. Some thirty-three exhibits were also entered into evidence, including a plan of Edey's yard submitted by the surveyor Thomas George Tyrer, photographs of the farm done by William A. Gale, the rifle identified as belonging to Hack, the pass book of his account at the Royal Bank in Neudorf, several articles identified as having belonged to Edey, and the receipts that Hack provided as proof of sale of the horses, wagon, and equipment.

The hearing resumed at 9:00 a.m. on the following day to hear from a further twenty-seven witnesses. Constables Bannerman and Watts related the course of their investigations, while Corporal J. Laight of the SPP Canora detachment, who was qualified as a handwriting expert, testified that the handwriting on the two receipts matched other documents written by Hack, but not documents known to have been written by Edey. H.B. Fairbairn, manager of the Royal Bank in Neudorf, produced records showing that Hack had approximately $2 in his savings account. Most of the remaining witnesses over the two days of the hearing were the local residents who had been interviewed during the police investigation, who were able to testify to Hack's whereabouts and movements both before and after the murder.

Anderson cross-examined most of the Crown witnesses. Of Dr. Findlay, he inquired whether some of Edey's wounds could have been accidentally inflicted by one of his horses. He briefly challenged Corporal Laight's testimony concerning the mismatch between Hack's and Edey's handwriting. Anderson's cross-examination of the local residents consisted largely of challenging their memory of specific dates or their ability to identify Edey's horses or other items that had belonged to the deceased. He called no witnesses of his own.

At the conclusion of the evidence, Matthews read a warning to the accused and then showed it to Hack: "Having heard the evidence, do you wish to say anything in answer to the charge? You are not obliged to say anything unless you desire to do so; but whatever you say will be taken down in writing and may be given in evidence against you at your trial." Hack replied, "I have nothing to say." Matthews then continued:

> This man is charged that he did commit murder. That is an indictable offence, and it is necessary to hold a preliminary hearing on a case of that kind. It is not for this court to decide whether he is guilty of this charge or not. It is my duty to decide as to whether I consider there is sufficient

evidence to connect this man with the charge or not, and if there was not sufficient evidence it would be my duty to discharge the prisoner, but on hearing the evidence, I find that there is evidence that in my opinion connects this man with the charge sufficiently to place him on his trial.

The hearing concluded at 5:00 p.m. on Tuesday 22 May and Matthews committed Hack to stand trial, whereupon he was again remanded in custody to Regina Jail. Trial was scheduled for the following October.

The preliminary inquiry provided Anderson with everything he needed to know about the case that the Crown would make against Hack at trial. As a result, he knew that there were no witnesses to the crime and no forensic evidence connecting his client to it – no bloodstains on his clothing or on his rifle. He therefore knew that the evidence against Hack was entirely circumstantial, primarily comprising (a) witnesses to his movements in the area of Edey's farm on the days leading up to the crime, (b) his possession of Edey's horses, wagon, and other items following the crime, (c) the allegedly forged receipts he produced to explain such possession, and (d) the false story he told of helping Edey move to Lorlie. Armed with this information, Anderson had more than four months to prepare an effective defence of his client.

# 3
# How Justice Can Miscarry

On 22 April 1985, Guy Paul Morin was arrested and charged with the murder of nine-year-old Christine Jessop. Christine had disappeared from her home in Queensville, Ontario, on 3 October 1984, after being dropped off by the school bus. Her body was not found until 31 December, more than thirty miles from her home. She had been sexually assaulted and stabbed to death. At Morin's trial in January 1986, the evidence connecting him to the crime consisted largely of hair and fibre samples and an alleged confession to two jailhouse informants. Morin was acquitted, which led the attorney general of Ontario to appeal the verdict, on the ground that the trial judge had wrongly instructed the jury on the standard of "reasonable doubt." The Court of Appeal agreed, and in June 1987, it ordered a new trial. At Morin's second trial, in May-June 1990, the Crown's evidence was bolstered by several witnesses who testified that his behaviour, both before Christine's disappearance and thereafter, had been "weird." This time the jury convicted.

Morin was assisted in appealing this verdict by a grassroots group calling itself the Association in Defence of the Wrongfully Convicted (AIDWYC). The appeal was intended to be based on the unreliability of the evidence presented at trial: the hair and fibre analysis, the testimony of the jailhouse informants, and the additional witnesses. However, mere days before the hearing was due to begin at the Ontario Court of Appeal, DNA test results came in that established conclusively that Morin was not the man who had sexually assaulted Christine. On 23 January 1995, the Court set aside Morin's conviction and entered an acquittal instead. Senior Crown counsel, and later the attorney general as well, conceded that Morin was innocent and apologized to him for the ten-year ordeal he and his family had undergone. In October 2020, Toronto police announced that they had finally been able to identify Christine Jessop's killer, a man who had died five years earlier.

A subsequent public inquiry into the Morin case identified four principal causes of the wrongful conviction: (a) "tunnel vision" on the part of police and prosecutors, who very early in the investigation began to focus exclusively on Morin as a suspect; (b) faulty scientific analysis of hair and fibres allegedly linking him to Christine; (c) reliance on the testimony of jailhouse informants (both trials), who had incentives to lie about his confession; and (d) the use of unreliable witness testimony (second trial).[1]

Morin's ordeal has come to serve, in the public's eye, as the very model of a wrongful conviction. There had been earlier such cases. One of the most notorious was that of Donald Marshall, Jr., the seventeen-year-old Mi'kmaq boy who, in 1971, was wrongly convicted of the murder of Sandy Seale. Marshall was acquitted by the Nova Scotia Court of Appeal in 1983, when a witness came forward testifying that they had seen another man stab Seale.[2] Other wrongful convictions would come after. Among the best known were those of Robert Baltovich, David Milgaard, Romeo Phillion, and Thomas Sophonow.[3] In each of these cases, the issue was the same: someone was convicted of a serious offence – usually murder – which they did not commit. This record of high-profile cases solidified the idea that a wrongful conviction is necessarily the conviction of someone who is factually innocent, as indicated by AIDWYC's later rebranding as Innocence Canada, with the mandate "to identify, advocate for, and exonerate individuals who have been convicted of a crime they did not commit and to prevent wrongful convictions through legal education and reform."[4]

Although this identification of wrongful conviction with factual innocence is common, it is also misleading because not every exoneration of the wrongfully convicted results in a finding of factual innocence. This was indeed the outcome in Morin's case, where DNA evidence could establish conclusively that he was not connected to the crime. But exonerating evidence of this definitive sort has not been available in every case of wrongful conviction.

On 30 September 1959, fourteen-year-old Steven Truscott was convicted of the sexual assault and murder of twelve-year-old Lynne Harper.[5] The evidence implicating him in the crime was largely circumstantial: he had given the girl a ride on his bicycle and was the last known person to have seen her alive. Evidence given at the trial by the forensic pathologist estimated that her death occurred at a time when she must have been in Truscott's company. Truscott was sentenced to death – the mandatory sentence for murder at the time – but the sentence was commuted to life imprisonment by the federal Cabinet. In 1966, partly as a result of Isabel LeBordais' book, *The Trial of Steven Truscott*,[6] the government referred the issue of whether Truscott had received a fair trial to the Supreme Court. In an 8–1 judgment, the Court decided that there had been no miscarriage of justice at the trial.[7]

In October 1969, Truscott was released on parole. There the matter rested until November 2001, when AIDWYC (as it then was) filed an appeal to have the case reopened. The minister of justice requested retired Quebec judge Fred Kaufman, who had led the 1998 commission inquiring into the wrongful conviction of Guy Paul Morin, to review this case. In October 2004, following Kaufman's report, the minister directed a Reference to the Ontario Court of Appeal to review whether new evidence would have changed the 1959 verdict. At that hearing, in June 2006, the court heard that the pathologist in the original trial had provided three different estimates of the time of Lynne Harper's death, the first two of which would have excluded Truscott as a suspect. Only after the police had narrowed their focus on Truscott did the pathologist testify definitively to the incriminating estimate. His alternative time estimates were concealed from both the defence and the court.

On 28 August 2007, having reviewed the entirety of the evidentiary record in the case, the Court of Appeal acquitted Truscott of the charges, concluding that "while it cannot be said that no jury acting judicially could reasonably convict, we are satisfied that if a new trial were possible, an acquittal would clearly be the more likely result."[8] However, in reaching this decision, the Court explicitly declined to issue a declaration of factual innocence. In Truscott's case, no DNA evidence existed, which could conclusively exclude him as the perpetrator of the sexual assault and murder. On 6 April 2006, the body of Lynne Harper had been exhumed by order of the attorney general of Ontario to test for DNA evidence, but no usable DNA was recovered from the remains. In the Court's view:

> The appellant has not demonstrated his factual innocence. To do so would be a most daunting task absent definitive forensic evidence such as DNA. Despite the appellant's best efforts, that kind of evidence is not available. The task of demonstrating innocence is particularly difficult in this case where in addition to the passage of almost a half-century since the crime, certain immutable facts cast some suspicion on the appellant. He was the last known person to see the victim alive and was with her at a location very close to where she was murdered. At this time, and on the totality of the record, we are in no position to make a declaration of innocence. Indeed, we are not satisfied that an acquittal would be the only reasonable verdict.[9]

For the record, even after the Court's decision, the Harper family continued to believe that Steven Truscott was responsible for Lynne's sexual assault and death.

The Truscott decision serves to remind us that the principal function of a court in a criminal case is to decide between conviction of the defendant and acquittal. While conviction necessarily implies a finding of factual guilt for the offence, acquittal does not similarly imply a finding of factual innocence. Instead, an acquittal is a determination that, based on the available evidence, the defendant's guilt could not be proven beyond a reasonable doubt. Courts are in the business of making decisions – conviction or acquittal – based on the evidence adduced at trial. Beyond that, they are not well positioned to decide the objective fact of the matter: whether or not the defendant actually committed the offence.[10] It was entirely consistent for the Court of Appeal to acquit Truscott on the ground that the full body of evidence, which was now available, would probably be insufficient to prove his guilt beyond a reasonable doubt, and to prescind from any finding concerning his factual innocence. In fact, the judges could have acquitted him while believing that, on a balance of probabilities, he actually did sexually assault and kill Lynne Harper (though they clearly did not believe that).

It is also possible for a Court of Appeal to overturn a murder conviction without entering an acquittal, if it holds that there was substantial unfairness in the original trial but cannot affirm that acquittal would be "the more likely result" in a new (or hypothetical) trial. This happened in 2009 in the case of Romeo Phillion, who was convicted in 1972 for the murder of Leopold Roy.[11]

Steven Truscott was almost certainly factually innocent. In that case, this was still an instance of a wrongful conviction in the usual sense: the conviction of someone for a crime they did not commit. But the linkage between wrongful conviction and factual innocence can be weakened even further. To see how, we need to ask the underlying question "What can render a conviction wrongful?" The popular conception applies a standard *external* to the judicial system: a conviction is wrongful whenever there is a mismatch between the legal outcome of a criminal trial (conviction) and the fact of the matter (the accused did not actually commit the offence in question). The same standard would yield an analogous category of wrongful acquittals of the factually guilty. On this conception, a conviction is *wrongful* whenever, due to failure of fit with the fact of the matter, it is *wrong*. There need have been no unfairness in the trial process itself: the verdict might have been entirely reasonable in light of the evidence adduced, but then put in question by further evidence (such as DNA) that becomes available only after the trial and is sufficient for exoneration.

The problem with this approach is that it treats "wrongful" as a purely factual, rather than normative, concept. However, ordinarily when we characterize an action as wrongful, we mean to say that it has *wronged* someone by treating them unjustly or unfairly or by violating their rights. Taking wrongfulness in this normative direction would point us towards looking for the defect – the wrongness or unfairness – in the judicial process that has resulted in the conviction of the accused, rather than the mismatch between that conviction and their factual innocence. Such a conception of a wrongful conviction would be purely *internal* to the judicial system: it would presuppose some violation of the right of the accused to a fair trial. In Truscott's case, such a violation occurred when the pathologist withheld from the defence and the court his alternative estimates of the time of death, two of which would have exonerated Truscott. Morin's right to a fair trial was compromised by the Crown's introduction of faulty hair and fibre evidence, its use of untrustworthy jailhouse informants, and its reliance on witnesses testifying to Morin's supposedly "weird" behaviour.

This internal standard of wrongfulness, by virtue of its focus on the fairness of the trial process itself, has the significant advantage that it can make sense of the wrongful conviction of the factually guilty.[12] On the external conception, this result is incoherent: if you were wrongfully convicted, then you must have been factually innocent. But the concept is not, in fact, incoherent. An accused who has indeed committed the offence in question can be wrongfully convicted of it if that conviction is the result of some procedural unfairness in the trial process. The unfairness could take any form: manufacturing of evidence, withholding of evidence from the defence, ineffective assistance of defence counsel, the trial judge's faulty charge to the jury, or whatever. All that would be necessary is that, *but for* that defect in the trial process, there is at least a reasonable probability that the accused would not have been convicted. A conviction resulting from any such defect would be *wrongful* by the internal standard, though not *wrong* by the external standard, because the accused actually did it.[13] It is also possible for a conviction to be wrongful by both the internal and external standards simultaneously: Donald Marshall was both factually innocent and, according to the 1989 report of a formal Commission of Inquiry into his case, the victim of ineffective assistance of counsel.[14]

Moving to an internal standard of wrongfulness could be highly significant for the case of Mike Hack. As may be clear already, and will become clearer later, Hack was almost certainly factually guilty of the murder of George Edey; he really did do it. Therefore, his conviction could not be considered wrongful by the external standard; there was no mismatch here between conviction and factual innocence. However, if his conviction was the result of significant unfairness in the trial process, then it might be wrongful after all.

There is another lesson to be learned from the Morin case: to fully capture the wrongfulness of a wrongful conviction, we need to widen our scope beyond the trial process itself. The mistakes made by the Crown during Morin's trial were the direct product of earlier faults in the criminal investigation into Jessop's murder, especially the tunnel vision of the investigating officers. Morin should never have been the principal – or sole – suspect in that murder. The concept of a wrongful conviction is too narrow to accommodate this broader field of focus. For that, we need the more inclusive notion of *miscarriage of justice*, which can take into account the entire criminal justice process, from initial investigation to trial outcome and beyond. In general, to say that a process has miscarried is to say that, due to some fault or defect, it has failed to reach its intended or proper outcome. In the case of pregnancy, the intended outcome is a live birth; in the case of a criminal investigation, it is justice according to the law. Therefore, a miscarriage of justice is said to have occurred whenever some fault or defect at any stage of the judicial process has a material effect on the justice of its outcome. By this logic, every wrongful conviction will be a miscarriage of justice, but not vice versa.

In Hack's case, the early stages of the criminal process seem to have been free of conspicuous failures or abuses. While it is true that Constables Bannerman and Watts narrowed the focus of their investigation to Hack almost immediately, and never considered any other possible suspect, they had sufficient reason to do so, since he was the one in possession of Edey's horses and wagon, with only an obviously suspect explanation of how he came by them. During questioning, all of which was witnessed by others, Hack was informed of his rights, and his deafness was accommodated by committing both questions and answers to paper. At no time does it appear that the suspect was harassed, intimidated, or deceived by the investigating officers. The autopsy and coroner's inquest produced a reliable reconstruction of the cause of Edey's death and a reliable estimate of its approximate time. The police officers carried out a thorough investigation, which involved interviewing dozens of witnesses, to collect the evidence linking Hack with that fateful night at Edey's farm. The preliminary inquiry performed its secondary function of fully informing the defence of the evidence to be adduced at trial, and Matthews' decision to commit the case to trial was fully justified in light of that body of evidence.

If we are to find any reason to suspect a miscarriage of justice in the case, the next place to look would be at the trial itself.

# 4
# October 1928

Founded in 1908 by the Grand Trunk Pacific Railway, the town of Melville was named after Charles Melville Hays, the then general manager of the railway, who four years later would perish on the *Titanic*. Melville's growth beyond that of other towns in the area came because of its designation as a divisional point by the railway. The town was also an important service centre for poultry, livestock, and grain farmers in the area. The population of Melville in 1928 was just under 3,000, and it would at no point in its subsequent history surpass 5,000. Nonetheless, it was incorporated as a city in 1960, and remains the smallest urban site in Saskatchewan with official city status.

The town's city hall was, and is, an imposing two-storey red brick and stone structure with a large central dome, which was built in 1912–13, partly at Hays's behest. The building was constructed in the Classical Revival architectural style, marked by its symmetrical form, decorative stone trim, and rounded-arch windows. It is a good example of the many combination town hall/opera houses that were built across Saskatchewan prior to the First World War, though its dome is unique in the province. Buoyed by the economic boom and the tremendous immigration to the prairies during the previous decade, and by a sense of optimism about the future, many of these communities, including Melville, erected buildings that surpassed their current and future needs. The town hall/opera houses became centres for both municipal administration and arts and cultural life in their communities. The ground floor of the Melville building was given over to various civic offices, while the second floor was dominated by a spacious auditorium that was used for public meetings and to mount operas and other forms of entertainment. It also served as the courthouse for the Court of King's Bench, Judicial District of Melville.

4.1. Melville city hall
Source: Saskatchewan Archives

The Court's fall 1928 sittings commenced on Tuesday 2 October. On the docket were eight criminal cases, including one for the theft of a dog. But the case that attracted the most attention was *Rex v. Hack*, which got underway on Wednesday 3 October. Melville had not seen a murder trial for ten years, not since Barney Belcourt, a twenty-seven-year-old forest ranger, was convicted of the murder of Florence Beatty, a mother of four, in October 1918. Belcourt had been living with Beatty and her husband Edward and had become infatuated with their twelve-year-old daughter Thelma. When his expressions of interest in her were rebuffed, Belcourt took advantage of Edward's absence on the night of 3 September to beat Florence brutally on the head with a blunt instrument and abduct Thelma, whom he then raped several times. Curiously, Belcourt's death sentence was commuted to life imprisonment, largely on the basis of a recommendation of mercy by Judge James McKay.[1]

Long before the 2:00 p.m. start time for Hack's trial, every available seat in the auditorium was occupied, with approximately two hundred spectators following the proceedings. Local high school students also drifted in after school let out at 4:00 p.m. Newspapers in Melville, Yorkton, Regina, and Saskatoon had been following the case since

4.2. Portrait of Donald Maclean
Source: University of Saskatchewan

Hack's arrest and preliminary inquiry, and they now reported daily on the progress of the trial. The case seems to have attracted little or no attention outside Saskatchewan.

Presiding was Justice Donald Maclean. Originally from Nova Scotia, Justice Maclean had been educated at Dalhousie University before moving to Saskatchewan in 1909. From 1917 to 1921, he served as the member of the Legislative Assembly for the riding of Saskatoon City;

for the last three of those years, he was leader of the Conservative Party and of His Majesty's Loyal Opposition. He left politics in 1921, when he was appointed to the Court of King's Bench. He taught in the Faculty of Law at the University of Saskatchewan until 1923, and later in the 1940s served as the University's chancellor and received an honorary doctorate of civil law. By 1928, he was a veteran of criminal trials, though this was his first capital case.

As at the preliminary inquiry, Ernest Gerrand appeared for the Crown, though he was now joined by Herbert E. Sampson, KC, from the attorney general's office in Regina, who had also prosecuted Belcourt ten years earlier. Sampson served as a Crown prosecutor in Saskatchewan for thirty-five years and had a reputation for a formidable memory, which enabled him to listen to evidence for days at a time and then apparently without notes ask essential questions that struck directly at the heart of the case. He took the lead both in opening and closing remarks and in examining the many witnesses. As before, William Elliott and Percy Anderson appeared for the accused. Sampson and Anderson had a history as adversaries prior to 1928, having appeared in five cases at the Court of Appeal, in which Sampson acted for the Crown and Anderson for the accused. (Eleven years later, Justice Anderson of the Court of King's Bench would preside over a murder trial in which Sampson appeared as the Crown attorney.)[2]

Hack was described in the press as about five feet eight inches in height and weighing approximately 160 pounds. "He is broad shouldered, inclined to be stout and of the husky type of Saskatchewan farmer of Austrian extraction. The accused is a clean-shaven man with a fairly determined looking jaw and somewhat intelligent face."[3] The charge was read that "he, the said Mike Hack, at or near the south-west quarter of Section 2 in Township 22 and Range 9 west of the second meridian, in the Province of Saskatchewan, did on or about the second day of May, 1928 murder George Edey." Upon his arraignment, Hack pleaded "not guilty." Hack sat in the prisoner's box during the subsequent proceedings, keeping his eyes for the most part on the judge.

In Saskatchewan, a trial before a jury was mandatory for a murder charge. In this case, a supplementary list of jurors was found to be necessary, and an additional thirteen jurors were, by order of the court, subpoenaed by the sheriff and added to the jury list. As Anderson challenged prospective jurors, Hack leaned over the rail of the box and scrutinized the list that his counsel held in his hand. He looked in turn at the jurors as they came up to be sworn. Once the jury was duly impanelled, Sampson outlined the case for the Crown. On the application of Anderson, the Crown witnesses he wanted excluded were named, upon which they left the courtroom. This was standard procedure to prevent later witnesses from tailoring their testimony to evidence given by earlier witnesses.

The Crown this time called forty-four witnesses and entered some twenty-eight exhibits into evidence. Because of Hack's deafness, four court reporters worked in fifteen-minute relays transcribing the evidence in shorthand, typing it up, and then passing it to him for his perusal. This procedure was highly unusual, as ordinarily a transcript of the evidence was not prepared until all of it had been heard, and then only in the event of an appeal or an application for clemency to the Department of Justice. It was expected that this work of transcription would hamper the progress of the trial, but the reporters managed to run just one hour behind the oral evidence. Hack sat motionless as the evidence unfolded, apparently oblivious to all around him. Leaning on the right rail of the prisoner's box, he provided verbal answers to his lawyers as they wrote out questions for him at intervals.[4]

Most of the evidence over the three days of the trial replicated what had been presented at the preliminary inquiry. The Crown opened its case by entering into evidence the plan of Edey's farmyard, created by Thomas Tyrer, and the photograph taken by William Gale. Constable Bannerman then recounted his investigation into Edey's disappearance, including his encounter with Hack on the road and his discovery of Edey's body on his own farm. Harold Fairbairn of the Royal Bank branch in Neudorf testified that Hack had a balance of $1.92 in his savings account as of 18 April 1928 and had subsequently made no deposits.

The evidence implicating Hack in Edey's murder was entirely circumstantial. There were no witnesses to the crime, and no forensic evidence was introduced linking the accused to the crime: no bloodstains on his clothing or his rifle, no fingerprints anywhere in Edey's house or barn, and no footprints in the farmyard or the manure pile. The absence of bloodstains could be explained by the fact that Hack was not apprehended until nearly a week after the fact, so he had had plenty of time to remove any incriminating marks. But there may not have been any stains to start with. The bleeding caused by the blows to Edey's head was largely intracranial; it was, in fact, the pressure from the internal bleeding on the brain that was the immediate cause of death. No blood was found in the loft, or anywhere else in the barn, and even when Edey's body was discovered in the manure pile, having lain there for six days, only a small amount of blood had pooled beneath his head, causing a clot of saturated straw to adhere to it.

By the 1920s, fingerprinting was well established in Canada as a means of identification, having supplanted an earlier system relying on a combination of various bodily measurements, such as height, breadth, and circumference of head, length of ear, length of thumb and forefingers, etc.[5] The newer system had been adopted by both the RCMP and the SPP, and Hack was duly fingerprinted upon his arrest. However, there is no indication that the investigating officers attempted to establish Hack's presence in Edey's house or barn by this means.

The Crown relied instead on the testimony of various residents in the vicinity of Edey's farm, who described Hack's movements about the area during the time in question, which established his presence at the farm on 1 May. These residents also testified to Hack's later possession of Edey's horses, wagon, equipment, and personal possessions. When he chose to cross-examine these witnesses, Anderson challenged their ability to recollect key dates and to identify Edey's possessions, probed for inconsistencies between their testimony at trial and their evidence given at the preliminary inquiry, and tried to suggest that they had colluded in their testimony. The following interrogation of Arthur Edey, brother of George, was typical. Arthur had testified that a fur coat, found in Hack's possession and entered into evidence, was the one he had given his brother in 1921.

Q. You haven't seen George since '21?
A. No, that is in '21.
Q. And the last time you saw that coat was in '21?
A. Well, last spring, yes. The last time I saw it was last in Duff.
Q. But before that?
A. In '21.
Q. That is a matter of some seven or eight years?
A. Seven years ago, anyway.
Q. All right, seven; and all you can say is that that looks like it, this fur coat looks like the same kind of fur?
A. Yes, the same kind of fur all right, and it is the same coat too.
Q. What distinguishing mark on it makes you think it is his coat?
A. Well, there are one or two distinguishing marks on it.
Q. What are they?
A. Down the front part of it is lighter fur than the rest part, and always was from the time I bought the coat. There is a front on there just the same as when I bought it.
Q. And what else?
A. The trademark on the coat is a Moose Head.
Q Well, I suppose the same Company that made the coat made many another coat with the Company's brand on it - the same brand?
A Well, I guess they would have.

Q. Calgary beer bottles all have the same trademark on them. You couldn't distinguish one Calgary beer bottle from the others?
A. No, but I could distinguish the beer if I got it.
Q. Well, that is the only way you are able to distinguish it?
A. No, there's another one yet.
Q. What is that?
A. There's a mark on the leather in the sleeve which was chewed by a mouse – the leather in the right-hand sleeve.
Q. Where?
A. In the armpit. I left it in the stable and the mice chewed it.
Q. Just chewed it once?
A. They did not chew it again because I never left it another night for them to get at it. That is the same coat. And I know that coat as well as I knowed my brother George.

The foregoing line of questioning might be classified as merely pointless, because Hack had been found in possession of horses and wagon that had undeniably belonged to Edey, and he was in any case on trial for murder, not theft. However, some other interrogations crossed the line to entirely frivolous, as in this extended exchange with Harry Towns, a storekeeper in Lorlie who knew Edey well from the time the latter had previously farmed near the town. Towns testified that, to his knowledge, Edey had not been in Lorlie since 1922 and had no intention of moving there.

Q. You do not seriously tell us that you knew the business of all the people in Lorlie?
A. No, I do not know their business.
Q. And he might have been coming to live with somebody in Lorlie and you not know anything about it?
A. It is possible, but I do not think he did.
Q. But did you know if he made any arrangement to go and live with anybody in Lorlie?
A. Not that I knew of. I enquired, and they did not know.
Q. But from those who you did not enquire of?
A. But they did not know him and had no place to provide him with.
Q. But all you know is that you did not see him there?
A. I did not see him.
Q. And do you mean to tell me that George Edey has not been in Lorlie since 1922?
A. Not to my knowledge.
Q. You are not sitting on the housetop watching him?

A. No.
Q. He might have been in Lorlie a dozen times and you not see him?
A. It is possible, but I do not think he was.
Q. You are not a sort of official recorder of the times everybody goes to Lorlie?
A. No.
Q. And he could have gone there lots of times and you not know of it?
A. He could have gone there in the nighttime.

HIS LORDSHIP: It does not matter whether Mr. Edey went to Lorlie or not. I do not see why we should bother about that.

Q. You say he could not have been in Lorlie and you not see him?
A. It is possible.

HIS LORDSHIP: Is the matter relevant?

MR ANDERSON: No, my lord.

Justice Maclean's evident exasperation with this line of questioning was understandable. The story that Hack told of Edey moving to Lorlie was intended to provide an explanation of his disappearance. Once Edey turned up in his own farmyard, very much dead, that story lost all its credibility. Therefore, Towns's testimony on direct examination seemed hardly relevant, except to establish the lengths to which Hack was prepared to go to conceal his crime. Hence, his questioning under cross-examination was even less relevant. It should be noted that this exchange occurred after Maclean had asked both counsel "not to enter into matters that are not really relevant."

Anderson devoted most of his attention to the Crown's two expert witnesses, who were the last to appear on Friday 5 October. Dr. C.A. Findlay once again testified that the cause of Edey's death was intracranial hemorrhage due to blows to the head by a blunt instrument inflicted several days earlier. In cross-examination, Anderson first attempted to probe whether Edey's injuries might have been inflicted by one of his horses.

Q. Now, these wounds could have been caused by a horse's hoof, couldn't they?
A. I suppose that individually they could have been caused by a horse's hoof. Any one of them could have been produced by it.

HIS LORDSHIP: You imply, I take it, that all these wounds would not have been produced by one impact of the horse's hoof?

WITNESS: Certainly not.

HIS LORDSHIP: It would require several impacts for each one of those cuts?

WITNESS: It would require an impact for each, for the first wound, the cross-shaped wound, it would require two.

Q. You think the deceased would have had to have been hit four times, practically, two over the top and one for each side?
A. One for each side, and one for each of the bruises.

When this line of questioning seemed to be going nowhere, Anderson next focused on Findlay's estimated time of death. Quoting several times from medical/legal textbooks, he posed a lengthy, and rather bizarre, series of questions to Findlay concerning the onset and duration of rigor mortis, none of which appeared to discredit the pathologist's expert opinion.

The Crown called a second expert witness at the trial, one who had not testified at the preliminary inquiry. The most incriminating evidence against Hack was his possession of Edey's horses, wagon, collars, and harnesses on 2 May and thereafter. Hack's account, as told to Constables Bannerman and Watts, was that he had purchased these items from Edey on 26 April and taken them away on 30 April. When the constables questioned Hack on 8 May, he was able to show them receipts, dated 26 April, for the purchase of the horses, wagon, and equipment. If these receipts were genuine, they would support his account, though it would still have to be explained how some of Edey's neighbours could have seen him in his field with his horses as late as the evening of 1 May. But were the receipts genuine?

Both the constables thought not. Upon being shown the receipts during his initial interview of Hack on 8 May, Constable Bannerman immediately concluded that they were "fictitious" and written by Hack himself. During the same interview, Constable Watts asked Hack to write out Edey's name and the amount he had paid Edey for the horses. Hack wrote the amount as "seven hundret dollars" and the name as "Geo. Adey," in each case matching the receipts. To Constable Watts' eyes, the handwriting was identical to that on the receipts. From the outset, then, the investigating officers concluded that the receipts were forgeries. If so, that fact would be highly incriminating, for Hack would be in a position to know that Edey could not contradict his account of the sale of the horses only if he knew that Edey was dead. And the most likely way he would know that was that he had killed him.

However, neither constable was a handwriting expert. If the Crown wished to establish that the receipts were forged, then it would need an expert witness willing to testify to this effect. At the preliminary inquiry, this role had been played by Corporal Laight, of the SPP Canora detachment, who had compared the handwriting of Edey and Hack and had concluded that the receipts were written by Hack. For the trial, Sampson did not call upon Laight but instead enlisted the services of Herbert J. Walter, a handwriting expert from Winnipeg.[6] Walter was given some four hundred cheques written by Edey to compare with the handwriting on the receipts. Enlarged photographs of these documents were shown and explained to the jury. In every one of them, Edey signed his name as "George Edey," including on a note dated on the same day as the receipts. Walter also offered the opinion that Edey had learned to write in England and that his handwriting was typically English in paying more attention to the formation of letters than to speed in writing. On the other hand, Hack's handwriting was a more speedy and connected style, typical of those who learned their penmanship in Canada. This handwriting and that on the two receipts allegedly written and signed by Edey were, in Walter's opinion, identical.

In cross-examination, Anderson did his best to emphasize that Walter's opinion that the receipts were in Hack's handwriting was just that – an opinion – and that opinions, even expert ones, could be mistaken:

Q. I suppose you have sometimes been wrong?
A. I do not pretend to be infallible, but I think in this case, the conclusion can be come to without a reasonable doubt.
Q. Isn't this one of the funny things about experts, one will get up and say, yes, that is the fellow's signature, and the other will get up and say, no, it is not?
A. In some cases, there are legitimate causes for a difference of opinion. In other cases, with qualified experts there should be an agreement.
Q. It is not what there should be, but what is?
A. There usually is with experts.
Q. You say you have been in Courts?
A. Yes.
Q. And you have had lots of experience?
A. Yes.
Q. Now, haven't you got up in Court and said: I think that is the fellow's signature, and another expert got up and said, I do not think it is at all, eh?

A. That is upon the reasons the experts give for their opinion whether they are the same or not.
Q. Haven't you had that experience?
A. I have been opposed in Court.
Q. You said one thing, and the other expert said another?
A. It is for the Court to decide whether the reasons given are reasonable or unreasonable.
Q. But the fact is that these experts almost proverbially disagree with you?
A. I know of one expert who has not been opposed in fourteen consecutive times.
Q. Where does he live – in Paradise?
A. No, he lives in New York.

Anderson did not, of course, call a handwriting expert who might have contradicted Walter's opinion. In the end, Walter stuck to his testimony, whose credibility Anderson did little to dispel.

The Crown's evidence in the case was concluded at 12:30 p.m. on Friday 5 October, the third day of the trial. Anderson announced that the defence would not be calling any witnesses, and the court was then adjourned until 3:00 p.m. so that the final transcript of the evidence could be prepared. There was then a delay while Hack read through the transcript. The jurors entered the courtroom at 3:15 p.m., followed by Justice Maclean about a half-hour later. The judge asked for the prisoner, and Anderson said that he was still occupied reading the last evidence that had been transcribed early that afternoon. Hack then entered the courtroom shortly before 4:00 p.m. But more dramatic was the entrance of his mother Dorothea, attired in black and wearing the traditional shawl of her native land. She kept her eyes on her son, just to her left in the prisoner's box as she sat in the front row. Tears sprang to her eyes occasionally and she had difficulty suppressing her emotions.

Because he had called no witnesses, Anderson had the privilege of addressing the jury last, a reversal of the usual order. Starting at 4:00 p.m., Sampson occupied an hour and a quarter in his closing remarks, outlining the many strands in the evidence that had been presented, which, though circumstantial, clearly connected Hack to the crime. Sampson also stressed the importance of the handwriting evidence, which showed that the receipts proffered by Hack had been forged. Anderson then took about an hour, emphasizing how the Crown's case rested entirely on "probabilities." He also said that the strongest evidence for the defence was Dr. Findlay's admission that Edey's injuries could have been caused by one of his horses. He concluded by reminding the jurors that, while they might find the defence's theory of Edey's death less probable than that of the Crown, the accused was entitled to the benefit of any reasonable doubt. He should therefore be acquitted, because the Crown had not succeeded in proving his guilt beyond reasonable doubt.

When the court resumed at 8:15 p.m., Justice Maclean commenced his charge to the jury. Jury trials are a division of labour between the judge, who is authoritative on matters of law, and the jurors, who must reach agreement on findings of fact. Justice Maclean's remarks began by outlining this division of labour and emphasizing the burden on the Crown of establishing guilt "beyond a reasonable doubt." He then made it clear to the jurors that should they find that Hack killed Edey, their verdict must be that he is guilty of murder. In 1928, the *Criminal Code* defined murder (in part) as culpable homicide "(a) if the offender means to cause the death of the person killed; or (b) if the offender means to cause to the person killed any bodily injury which is known to the offender to be likely to cause death, and is reckless whether death ensues or not."[7] Justice Maclean emphasized that in Hack's case, there could be no ground for a verdict of a lesser offence, such as manslaughter.[8] The cause of Edey's death made it quite clear that whoever struck him multiple times on the head either intended to kill him or, at the very least, knew that the blows were likely to have this effect. Therefore, as Justice Maclean put the point, "If you find him guilty at all, it must be guilty of murder. And if you do not find him guilty of murder, you cannot find him guilty of anything else; it is either murder or acquittal."

Most of the remainder of the charge consisted of the judge's comments on the evidence, intended as guidance to the jury as they work their way through it. In assessing these comments, it may help to recall the prosecution's theory of the crime. In summary:

> Mike Hack owned a half-section of land near Dubuc but, lacking both horses and equipment, had no means to farm it. George Edey had a reputation in the area for having the finest horses, so Hack decided that he must have Edey's horses. On 1 May, Hack stayed overnight at Edey's farm and was allowed to sleep in the hayloft. Sometime around midnight, Edey went to the barn to feed his horses. When he climbed the ladder to the loft to pitch hay down to the mangers, Hack struck him on the back of the head with the butt of his rifle, and continued hitting him until Edey was dead. Hack dragged the body from the barn to the manure pile and buried it under some straw. He then hitched two of Edey's horses to the wagon, tied two others behind, and set out on the road, ending up that evening at the farm

of his sister Dora and George Hepting. Sometime thereafter, while staying at his mother's place, Hack used her receipt book to forge receipts for the horses, wagon, and equipment, dating them to 26 April.

According to this theory, Hack was guilty of murder, theft, and forgery. For its part, the defence put forward three rival theories:

1. Mike Hack bought the horses and wagon from George Edey on 26 April and took them away on 30 April. Edey's subsequent death was caused by injuries inflicted either by one of his horses or by a person or persons unknown. Hack's receipts for purchase of the horses and wagon were genuine.
2. Mike Hack bought the horses and wagon from George Edey on 26 April and took them away on 30 April. Edey's subsequent death was caused by injuries inflicted either by one of his horses or by a person or persons unknown. Sometime thereafter, having heard of Edey's disappearance, Hack realized that he needed proof of purchase and so forged the receipts.
3. George Edey's death was caused by injuries inflicted either by one of his horses or by a person or persons unknown. Sometime thereafter, Hack came to Edey's farm, took away the horses and wagon, and forged the receipts.

According to these theories, Hack was guilty either of nothing at all, or of forgery alone, or of theft and forgery. In none of these three theories was he guilty of murder.

The jury's task was to determine whether the Crown had proven its theory beyond a reasonable doubt or, alternatively, whether any of the theories of the defence had succeeded in raising such a doubt. As far as cause of death was concerned, Justice Maclean suggested that the jury "will have no difficulty in coming to [the] conclusion" that Edey died as a result of repeated blows to the head and that these blows could not have been self-inflicted. He then cast doubt on the defence's theory that the blows could have been inflicted by one of Edey's horses: "Is that reasonable, or is it mere groundless or fantastic theory?" The clincher, at least in the judge's mind, was that "at any rate, the horse did not bury him." Justice Maclean as much as directed the jury to find that Edey died as a result of human agency. The only real question for them to decide then was: Whose agency?

The judge then turned to the fact that the evidence connecting Hack to the crime was entirely circumstantial. The jury must first decide whether to believe the evidence offered in testimony by the various witnesses. If so, then they must further determine whether that evidence supports the conclusion that Hack was the killer beyond a reasonable doubt: "That is to say, the circumstances must not only be consistent with [that] conclusion ... but must be inconsistent with any other reasonable theory." The jury, Justice Maclean suggested, will "have no difficulty coming to [the] conclusion" that Hack was in possession of Edey's horses on 2 May. If so, then they must decide whether the receipts that Hack proffered for the sale of the horses and equipment were genuine. While pointing out that the jury need accept the testimony of the handwriting expert only if he "gives good reason for his opinion," the judge also emphasized the differences between Hack's handwriting and that of Edey. Should the jury find that Hack forged those receipts, then they will need to ask why he would have done so. They may conclude that he needed to explain his possession of the horses and knew that Edey would not be able to contradict his story as he knew that Edey was dead, and he knew this because he had killed him and concealed the body. "Do you spell out from that story that the accused manufactured, with the knowledge that Edey was dead and buried, and if he had that knowledge, can you find any reasonable theory on which to explain it other than that he was the man who did the killing?"

Justice Maclean concluded his charge by acknowledging the elephant in the room. Under the terms of the 1927 *Criminal Code*, three offences carried the death penalty: murder, treason, and rape. Capital punishment was never imposed for rape in Canada and was officially abolished for this offence in the 1954 revision of the *Code*. Between 1867 and 1976, when the death penalty was abolished, 705 people were hanged in Canada, all but one for murder.[9] (The exception was Louis Riel, condemned to death for treason.) Despite the fact that through the twentieth century, public opinion in Canada consistently favoured capital punishment for murder,[10] some attempts at abolition had been made as early as the 1910s. In the House of Commons, the abolitionist movement was led by Robert Bickerdike, who served from 1900 to 1917 as the Liberal member for the Montreal riding of St. Lawrence.[11] Bickerdike opposed the death penalty on moral and religious grounds, but also because, as he contended, it was administered disproportionately to the poor. Every year from 1914 to 1917, he introduced a private member's bill in the abolitionist cause, each of which was handily defeated. He was also a founder and president of the National Prison Reform Association, established in 1916, which merged three years later with the Honour League of Canada to become the Canadian Prisoners' Welfare Association. This body lobbied against capital punishment and in favour of prison reform. As it happens, Bickerdike had a historical interest in the matter of the death penalty. His ancestor and namesake, a member of a prominent Yorkshire family, was executed in 1585 for the crime of being Catholic. From that point on, the eldest son of every branch of the Bickerdike family was named Robert.

In 1928, a judge had no sentencing discretion whatever after a murder conviction. Life imprisonment became available as a penalty only much later, in 1961, when the offences of capital and non-capital murder were distinguished.[12] In any case, at least based on the prosecution's theory, Hack's killing of Edey would then have qualified as capital murder, since it was not only intentional but also "planned and deliberate." As noted earlier, during the week before the killing, Hack had told various people that he had purchased four horses from a farmer around Duff. Clearly, he intended to acquire Edey's horses by one means or another and, given that he had no funds to buy them, only one means was available to him. In any case, the jury had to be made aware that a finding of guilt would be followed swiftly by a sentence of death (though not necessarily by death itself: as we will see later, fewer than half of all death sentences imposed in Canada actually culminated in a hanging). Justice Maclean made sure that the jurors were aware of that fact, and then exhorted them to ignore it: "The law is there and we have to administer it. You have your part and I have mine. And you must do your part fearlessly, impartially, and no weak sentiment should come in and influence you when you have the facts."

Neither Sampson, for the Crown, nor Anderson, for the accused, registered any objection to the judge's charge. The jury duly retired at 8:50 p.m. and returned at 10:35 p.m. to announce a verdict of "guilty." Hack's lawyers had arranged for his mother Dorothea to leave the court before the verdict was read, despite her reluctance to do so. Justice Maclean moved directly to sentencing: "The Jury have found you guilty. There is only one sentence that I can impose; and the sentence of the Court is that you shall be taken from here and be conveyed to the Provincial Gaol at or near Regina and be there confined until the 9th day of January, 1929, and on that day be taken to the gallows there and there be hanged by the neck until you are dead; and may mercy be shown you." The sentence was copied in longhand by one of the court reporters, and Hack stood in the prisoner's box to read it. "Composed and strangely quiet until the last, Hack expressed no emotion as he learned that he was to die."[13]

# 5
# The Roads Not Taken

Since Mike Hack was not factually innocent, his murder conviction could be wrongful, and thus a miscarriage of justice, only if there was some serious failure or defect in the trial process. To determine whether this was the case, we need to look at the various players in that process: the prosecution, the judge, the jury, and the defence.

There seems to have been no wrongdoing on the part of the prosecution. Herbert Sampson led basically the same body of factual evidence that had been presented at the preliminary inquiry, with pretty much the same list of witnesses, except for swapping in one handwriting expert for another. The Crown's case was built carefully and methodically, and there was little that Percy Anderson was able to do in cross-examination to dislodge it.

As for Justice Maclean's conduct of the trial, there is nothing in the record to indicate an animus or bias against the defendant. The obvious place to look for procedural unfairness would be his charge to the jury, in which the judge all but directed the jurors *not* to find that the blows that killed George Edey were inflicted by one or more of his horses. They were therefore to attribute his death to human agency, and only one human agent was found in possession of Edey's horses and wagon after the killing, with receipts, which a handwriting expert had testified were forged. Of course, Justice Maclean repeatedly reminded the jurors that they, and not he, were the finders of fact and that they were free to disregard any comments he might offer on the evidence: "Those comments ... are merely intended to be helpful to you, and if they do not appear to you to be well founded in good reason, you will brush them aside. To my comments on the evidence, if I should happen to disclose any opinion one way or the other, you pay no attention unless you find good reason for it." Despite these disclaimers, however, when the jurors retired to their deliberations, they must have known very well the finding of fact that the judge was expecting from them.

Did the trial judge overstep the mark here? The Ontario Court of Appeal has stated that "a jury charge should be even-handed, the instructions fair and balanced. A jury charge should not be a partisan broadcast ... The purpose of a jury charge is to educate the decision-maker so that it will make an informed decision, not to tell the decision-maker what decision to make."[1] Justice Maclean's charge stuck pretty well to this script, though the prosecution's theory of the crime was treated as a good deal more credible than any of the theories proffered by defence counsel. In fairness, however, the prosecution's theory *was* much more credible.

Although the evidence implicating the accused in this case was entirely circumstantial, it was also quite conclusive. During his cross-examination of Dr. Findlay, Anderson tried to probe the possibility that the injuries were the result of a fall or had been inflicted by a horse. But the fact that at least six different blows were struck to Edey's head made all of these alternative scenarios seem merely fantastical. Anderson also challenged Findlay on time of death, evidently hoping to disconnect the fatal event from the time of Hack's known presence at the Edey farm. But that ploy did not work either. Finally, the theory that someone else had killed Edey also lacked all credibility, since there was no plausible alternative suspect. Only Hack had been seen roaming about in the vicinity in the days before the killing, while carrying a rifle. Only Hack had been seen approaching Edey's farm on the previous day. And only Hack had been seen the next day with the horses and wagon. There was simply no one else to whom the crime could reasonably be attributed. So even if Justice Maclean improperly led the jury to their finding of fact (and it is far from clear that he did), it very likely made no difference. Any twelve reasonable men (they were, of course, all men) would have come to the same conclusion as the judge, based on all this evidence.

When we turn to the jury, we need to ask whether ethnic animosity could have had any bearing on their verdict. Though Hack was born in Saskatchewan, his parents were ethnic Germans who had emigrated from the Austro-Hungarian Empire. Edey was a more recent immigrant from England. The trial was held in the northern part of the Pheasant Hills region, where the residents were predominantly British, many of them descendants of the settlers imported in the latter decades of the previous century by the Primitive Methodist Colonization Company. By contrast, residents in the Lemberg-Neudorf area farther south tended to be ethnic Germans. Hence, this killing, at least based on the prosecution's theory, crossed ethnic lines. Alone among the newspapers covering the trial, the Melville *Advance* listed the names of the twelve jurors. Almost all of them were recognizably British.

There were precedents for jury verdicts in murder trials being swayed against the accused because of strong community hostility. One of the most striking occurred more than forty years earlier. In the evening of 21 December 1883, a farm implement salesman named Peter Lazier was shot to death at the farmhouse of Gilbert and Margaret Jones, a few miles west of Picton, Ontario.[2] The ensuing police investigation quickly focused on three suspects – David Lowder, his brother George, and Joseph Thomset – who lived about five miles from the scene of the crime. All three were charged with murder and, in May 1884, stood trial at the Prince Edward County Courthouse in Picton. The case was similar in some respects to that of Hack. All three accused were local blue-collar workers: the Lowder brothers were mason and farm worker, respectively, while Thomset was a fisher. Furthermore, the principal evidence against the three accused was entirely circumstantial (and far less conclusive than the evidence connecting Hack to the murder of Edey). Notwithstanding the weakness of the Crown's case, George Lowder and Thomset were convicted of the murder and sentenced to death. The case against David Lowder was dismissed by the trial judge. What stood out about the case was the intensity of the local community's feelings against the accused:

> The community was out for blood and a hostile mood prevailed throughout the trial. The courtroom audience cheered the prosecution and jeered the defence, and in the evenings, hotel barroom patrons impatiently anticipated the hangings they so wanted to occur. The trial judge and the lawyers urged the jury of twelve men who determined the fate of the accused men to decide the case on the basis of the evidence and not be swayed by the community's hostility, but the jury took little time to convict.[3]

The locals got the hangings they wanted. Although the jury recommended mercy, the appeals for clemency were denied, and Lowder and Thomset were hanged on 10 June 1884. The community's strong feelings do not appear to have been ethnically based. Prince Edward County was heavily British, being home to many descendants of United Empire Loyalists. Peter Lazier was himself such a descendant, though the family had originally been Huguenots who came to America to escape persecution in France. The motive of the crime appeared to be robbery. Gilbert Jones had that very day received $555 (an enormous sum at the time) for the sale of a load of hops and had the cash in his farmhouse. The murder victim was an overnight visitor in the Jones home, thus a mere bystander during the attempted robbery. The community's intense reaction to the murder, and its thirst for blood, seemed rooted not in animosity specifically against the accused men, but in resentment that the tranquility of their remote and peaceable corner of the province had been shattered in such a senseless and violent way.[4]

In the extensive press coverage of Hack's trial, there was no suggestion of any such hostility on the part of the local Pheasant Hills community towards the accused. Aside from the reference to Hack's "Austrian extraction," the press covering the trial seemed to take little interest in his German heritage or in the fact that he was alleged to have killed an Englishman. The British residents in the area might have been expected to harbour some animosity towards Germans, given that it had been a mere ten years since the end of hostilities in the Great War, and only eight years since the Treaty of Versailles in January 1920 had officially concluded the conflict with Germany.

January 1920 also marked the end of the period during which the *War Measures Act* was in effect in Canada. The act, passed in August 1914 shortly after the war broke out, gave the federal Cabinet sweeping powers to suspend civil liberties and to govern by order-in-council. On 15 August, the government issued the *Proclamation Respecting Immigrants of German or Austro-Hungarian Nationality*, which authorized the arrest and detention of persons of these origins if there were "reasonable grounds" to believe they were "engaged or attempting to engage in espionage or acts of a hostile nature, or giving or attempting to give information to the enemy, or assisting or attempting to assist the enemy." During the war, more than 8,500 men, along with some women and children, were interned by the Canadian government. Most of the internees were recent immigrants from the western Ukrainian regions of Galicia and Bukovyna. They were held in twenty-four internment camps across the country, one of which was briefly located in Saskatchewan (near Saskatoon). Another 80,000 people, mostly Ukrainian Canadians, were obliged to register as "enemy aliens" during the war. They were compelled to report regularly to the police and were also subject to restrictions on their freedom of speech, as well as on their movements and associations.

Ostensibly intended to safeguard national security during the war, these measures also reflected the very strong anti-Ukrainian sentiment prevalent across the country during the pre-war era. Between 1891 and 1914, some 170,000 Ukrainian immigrants arrived in Canada, many of them attracted by the promise of free land in the west. These Eastern

European newcomers, however essential to the nation's developing industrial and agricultural economy, were regarded by many Canadians of British descent as dirty, inferior, "other" – prejudices that were expressed openly in newspapers and other forums, often in overtly Social Darwinist forms.[5]

Hack was thirteen years old when the war started, and seventeen when it ended. We know that he was not interned during the years when the *War Measures Act* was in force. In 1914, he attended school (sporadically); in 1916, he was confirmed in Trinity Lutheran Church in Lemberg; in 1919, he was charged with the theft of a horse and buggy in Neudorf. In fact, there is no evidence that any member of the Hack family was interned, despite the fact that Mathias and Dorothea were themselves immigrants from Galicia. Neither is there any indication that either they or their children were regarded with animosity by their British neighbours. Corporal Metcalfe, the RCMP officer who was involved in the investigation of Edey's murder, described the Hack family thus:

> Matt Hack [who died in August 1925] ... was considered by the citizens of the district, as being of very good reputation and character ... There has been 13 children born to the Hacks, 5 died of various diseases at the ages from one year to 27 years. 8 children are living and are married, and are considered good citizens ... Mike Hack's parents and his family are of good reputation and character in the district, they are very religious and attend the German Lutheran Church. Their homes are very neat and tidy and well kept, and are very clean in themselves.[6]

Corporal Metcalfe's math was slightly wrong. Of the eight surviving Hack children (as of 1928), seven were married and living on their own farms. Mike was the exception, never marrying or establishing a residence of his own.

The Hacks may have escaped the widespread anti-Ukrainian sentiment of the time in part because they were not newcomers, having been settled in the area since 1894. By the late 1920s, the Hack family, with its children now distributed over several farms, was better known and better established in the area than was George Edey, who arrived much more recently in 1914. Edey was a tenant of Luke Battersby rather than a landowner, was unmarried, lived alone, had no family in the area, and seems to have kept himself very much to himself. The Hacks may also have benefited by being ethnic Germans, rather than Slavs. Despite the fact that Germany was the official enemy during the war, many British subjects seem to have felt a closer kinship with the Protestant Germans from Ukraine than with the more "exotic" Orthodox Slavs.

There is also no evidence that Hack in particular was regarded by the locals with suspicion or hostility. As we shall see later, after his conviction, a number of residents in the area signed a petition asking for commutation of his death sentence. Based on the evidence of the petition, and also on affidavits by some of his neighbours, Hack was widely thought to be "queer" (in those days, synonymous with "odd" or "different"), but he does not seem to have been disliked.

In any case, a jury did not have to be motivated by bias against the accused to find Hack guilty on the basis of the evidence adduced at trial. Therefore, if we can find no fault with the prosecution, judge, or jury, this leaves us with the conduct of the defence.

One feature of the trial that might puzzle us now was its brevity. Because the stakes for the accused are so high, we are accustomed to murder trials lasting considerably longer. Since the stakes were even higher back when the death penalty was mandatory for a murder conviction, we may be surprised that this trial – from jury selection to verdict – wrapped up neatly in the space of three days. However, the Hack trial was not an outlier in this respect. In 1928, there were eighteen other murder trials in Canada that ended in convictions, of which only one lasted longer than three days. That was the Quebec trial of nineteen-year-old Bernard Rhéaume, accused of beating Hervé Dupont to death with a wrench. The trial lasted five days in October 1928 (overlapping with the Hack trial). Most of the remaining trials that year lasted either two or three days, with two of them even managing to run their course in a single day. This pattern of the relatively short duration of murder trials was quite stable over time. If we fast-forward thirty years to 1958, when the death penalty was still mandatory, we find twenty-one murder trials across the country ending in conviction. Of that total, two-thirds lasted fewer than five days, though a few did stretch on to nine days or more.[7]

The Hack trial moved along at a relatively brisk pace, considering that some forty-four witnesses were heard from over the three days, all of whose evidence had to be transcribed. But the defence counsel Anderson was partially responsible for maintaining this pace, since his cross-examination of most of the Crown witnesses was quite perfunctory, and he called no witnesses of his own. It is this last feature of his defence of Hack that may be the most puzzling. That no witnesses whatsoever should testify on behalf of the accused in a capital murder case might seem quite extraordinary.

But whom might Anderson have called? No one was in a position to furnish Hack with an alibi for the murder. He might have put family members or other local residents on the stand as character witnesses, but then it would have come to light under cross-examination that Hack had a troubled, and occasionally violent, history. According to Corporal Metcalfe, the accused "does not bear a very good character in the Neudorf District and has always been considered by the citizens as a petty thief, a liar, and a dangerous person to be at large in the community."[8] The impact on the jury of any testimony by those who knew him was unlikely to be favourable. That leaves only one person that Anderson might have called: Hack himself.

Until the latter part of the nineteenth century, defendants in Canadian criminal trials were prevented by law from testifying under oath in their own defence.[9] They were therefore afforded no opportunity to tell their own story or rebut the evidence given against them. However, this exclusion had been removed for all criminal trials in 1893, so Hack was quite free to take the witness stand. In light of the defence he was actually conducting, Anderson's decision not to call Hack seems entirely sensible. Hack's deafness would have made both direct examination and cross-examination cumbersome, because questions would have had to be put to him in writing. Furthermore, his story that he purchased the horses and wagon from Edey, that he last saw Edey on 30 April when he came to collect his purchases, and that he did not forge the receipts, had already been thoroughly undermined by the many Crown witnesses. He would have been reduced to stubbornly repeating that story under oath and would have been exposed to cross-examination by a very accomplished and resourceful Crown attorney, a process from which his credibility could not have emerged unscathed.

So perhaps Anderson just had no witnesses he could call after all. Alternatively, his decision to lead no defence evidence could have been strategic. Under the rules of trial procedure, once all evidence has been presented, the defence is normally called upon first to provide closing arguments, followed by the prosecution. This is the reverse of the speaking order at the beginning of the trial. However, there is an exception to this procedure when the defence has presented no witnesses, in which case it has the privilege of speaking last.[10] This provision was laid out explicitly in Section 661 of the 1892 *Criminal Code* and was in force at the time of Hack's trial. As the evidence against the accused was entirely circumstantial, Anderson may have felt that his best chance of securing an acquittal would be to have the opportunity to sow some seeds of doubt in the minds of the jurors shortly before they retired to consider their verdict.[11] A desperate measure, but *faute de mieux*. If this was indeed what he had in mind, then the strategy failed quite comprehensively because the jury took less than two hours to return with its verdict of guilty.

However this might be, there remains an alternative scenario in which putting Hack on the stand, along with others who knew him well, might have helped to make a point. But it would have required Anderson to pursue a quite different line of defence. The law allows a defendant numerous ways of mounting a defence against a criminal charge. The most straightforward is to maintain factual innocence and challenge the prosecution's evidence connecting the accused to the offence ("I didn't do it"). To the extent that Anderson undertook any defence of Hack, this was the tactic he attempted, though only through cross-examination of Crown witnesses and with scant success. But other options are available to defendants as well.[12] One is to admit having committed the act but claim a justification for doing so ("I did it, but it wasn't wrong"). Self-defence, for example, can serve as a justification for causing a person grievous bodily harm, or even killing them. Another option is to offer an excuse ("I did it, and it was wrong, but I am not culpable for having done it"). The point of an excuse is to show not that the offence committed by the accused was justified, but that they could not reasonably have been expected to avoid committing it. Provocation can serve as such an excuse, as can duress. Finally, there are what we may call defences of non-responsibility ("I did it, but I was not responsible for my actions").[13] Intoxication is one such defence, as is infancy. But the best-known defence of non-responsibility is insanity.

As early as the fourteenth century, English law recognized that it was improper to punish a person whose mentality did not allow them to have *mens rea* (a "guilty mind"), or to understand the difference between "good and evil."[14] But the conditions for a successful defence of insanity came to be formalized only much later, in 1843, when a Scottish woodturner named Daniel M'Naghten took a pistol and shot Edward Drummond, secretary to Sir Robert Peel, the British prime minister. M'Naghten had mistaken Drummond for Peel, whose Tory party M'Naghten believed to be responsible for a systematic campaign of persecution against him. When Drummond died five days later, M'Naghten was charged with his murder. At his trial, in May 1843 in the Central Criminal Court, the Old Bailey, he pleaded not guilty by reason of insanity. To support this plea, M'Naghten's defence counsel called nine medical experts to attest to the fact that he was not in a sound state of mind at the time of committing the act. The medical evidence brought forward stated that persons of otherwise sound mind might be affected by morbid delusions and that M'Naghten's conviction of persecution by the Tories was just such a delusion. It was argued that a person labouring under a delusion of this sort might usually possess an accurate sense of right and wrong, but in relation to acts connected to their delusion, they may lack such a sense.[15]

In relation to the charge against M'Naghten, Lord Chief Justice Tindal instructed the jury in the following terms:

> The question to be determined is, whether at the time the act in question was committed, the prisoner had or had not the use of his understanding, so as to know that he was doing a wrong or wicked act. If the jurors should be of opinion that the prisoner was not sensible, at the time he committed it, that he was violating the laws both of God and man, then he would be entitled to a verdict in his favour: but if, on the contrary, they were of opinion that when he committed the act he was in a sound state of mind, then their verdict must be against him.[16]

After brief deliberation, the jury acquitted M'Naghten on grounds of insanity. Immediately following the verdict, M'Naghten was transferred to the State Criminal Lunatic Asylum at Bethlem Hospital, where he spent the next twenty-one years. In 1864, he was moved to the newly opened Broadmoor Asylum, where he died a year later.

The verdict in M'Naghten's trial caused an outcry both among the public and in Parliament. As a result, five hypothetical questions relating to crimes committed by persons with delusions were put to a panel of judges of the Court of Common Pleas. Their answers to these questions were delivered to the House of Lords in June 1843. One of these answers became enshrined in law as the M'Naghten Rules for determining legal insanity:

> The jurors ought to be told in all cases that every man is to be presumed to be sane, and to possess a sufficient degree of reason to be responsible for his crimes, until the contrary be proved to their satisfaction; and that to establish a defence on the ground of insanity, it must be clearly proved that, at the time of the committing of the act, the party accused was labouring under such a defect of reason, from disease of the mind, as not to know the nature and quality of the act he was doing; or, if he did know it, that he did not know he was doing what was wrong.[17]

So formulated, the M'Naghten Rules contained four key elements:

1. The initial presumption is that the accused is sane; the defence must therefore prove the contrary to the jury's satisfaction;
2. For a defence of insanity to succeed, the accused must be shown to have had a "disease of the mind";

3. That disease of the mind must have caused a "defect of reason";
4. As a result of this defect of reason, the accused *either* did not know the nature and quality of their act *or* did not know that the act was wrong.

This fourth element sets out the two branches of the insanity defence; either, if made out, is sufficient for the defence to succeed. For the first branch, the defect of reason from which the accused is suffering must cause them not to understand what it is that they are doing. M'Naghten might, for instance, have suffered from the delusion that by shooting Drummond – or Peel – he was inoculating him against smallpox.[18] M'Naghten's defence, however, rested on the second branch: that his delusion of persecution led him not to know that shooting Drummond (or Peel) was wrong.

The M'Naghten Rules served as the common law test of insanity in Canadian criminal trials, both before and after Confederation, until their incorporation into the 1892 *Criminal Code* in the following form:

> 11(1) No person shall be convicted of an offence by reason of an act done or omitted by him when labouring under natural imbecility, or disease of the mind, to such an extent as to render him incapable of appreciating the nature and quality of the act or omission, and of knowing that such act or omission was wrong.[19]

This formulation of the rules was based on an 1879 British Draft Code developed by a Royal Commission, including the famed English jurist Sir James Fitzjames Stephen but never adopted there. The *Criminal Code* also preserved the presumption of sanity in the M'Naghten Rules: "Every one shall be presumed to be sane at the time of doing or omitting to do any act until the contrary is proved."[20] However, while the *Code* provisions were clearly intended to capture the spirit of the M'Naghten Rules, they departed from their letter in a number of respects, some of which were potentially important for the defence of Mike Hack.[21]

Under the M'Naghten Rules, a "disease of the mind" was the sole mental condition that could ground an insanity defence. The *Code* provisions added "natural imbecility" as a further qualifying condition. At least in their original formulation, the two conditions were importantly different. What "disease of the mind" suggests to us now is any (serious) form of mental illness or disorder. By 1980, the Supreme Court had given it this expansive definition:

> In summary, one might say that in a legal sense "disease of the mind" embraces any illness, disorder or abnormal condition which impairs the

human mind and its functioning, excluding however, self-induced states caused by alcohol or drugs, as well as transitory mental states such as hysteria or concussion. In order to support a defence of insanity the disease must, of course, be of such intensity as to render the accused incapable of appreciating the nature and quality of the violent act or of knowing that it is wrong.[22]

Reflecting the breadth of this definition, it is now canonical to speak of "the defence of mental disorder" rather than the insanity defence. In 1928, however, "disease of the mind" would likely have been interpreted much more narrowly. M'Naghten himself apparently suffered from "delusions," which suggests some kind of psychosis.

Unlike "disease of the mind," which, as the Supreme Court later acknowledged, is entirely a legal term of art, "imbecility" actually had considerable currency in the forensic psychiatry of the day. In common parlance nowadays, "imbecile," along with "moron" and "idiot," is simply an epithet hurled at someone alleged to be backward or stupid, although the case against the casual usage of these terms is growing strong.[23] But back then, these terms were used to mark degrees of (what was then known as) feeble-mindedness or mental retardation. In the late nineteenth and early twentieth centuries, research into this condition was driven in large measure by the developing field of eugenics, first labelled as such by Francis Galton in 1883 and later advanced by psychologists like Henry Herbert Goddard.[24] The two central tenets of eugenics were that feeble-mindedness was a major cause of many social ills – including crime, drunkenness, indigence, and sexual degeneracy – and that it was heritable. Therefore, in the interest of improving social conditions, it was essential to be able to both identify the segment of the population who suffered from this condition and to prevent them from procreating. The preventive measures advocated by the eugenics movement included prohibiting the feeble-minded from marrying, segregating them in institutions, and subjecting them to involuntary sterilization.

Since feeble-mindedness admitted of degrees, it was thought to be important to develop some reasonably precise means of measuring the condition. For this purpose, researchers turned to the intelligence tests devised in 1905 by Albert Binet and Theodore Simon. The Binet–Simon IQ tests scored subjects on their performance at some thirty diverse tasks, including recognition of objects, recall of phrases, and combining words into a sentence. Results from these tests were combined into a single grade on a normalized scale on which a score of 100 represented average intelligence. Scores below the norm were correlated with three degrees of feeble-mindedness: moron (mildly subnormal = 50–75), imbecile (moderately subnormal = 25–50), and idiot (extremely subnormal = <25).[25] Since these categories were delineated only later, the phrase "natural imbecility" in the 1892 *Code* must be read as referring to feeble-mindedness (or what we would now call intellectual disability or cognitive impairment) generally, and not specifically to its moderate variety. A disability of this sort was obviously thought by the framers of the *Code* to be different from any form of mental illness or psychosis.

In the M'Naghten Rules, the "disease of the mind" must result in the accused not knowing either the nature and quality of their act or the fact that it is wrong. In the *Code* formulation, that condition must deprive the accused of the *capacity* to know these things. This wording suggests that what the insanity defence requires is not merely some episodic failure of knowledge but an underlying defect of reason. This would be even clearer for the companion condition of "natural imbecility," where the cognitive impairment would be expected to deprive its subject of the ability to form the requisite kind of knowledge.

Additionally, under the *Code* rules, the perpetrator must lack the capacity not merely to *know* the nature and quality of their act but also to *appreciate* it. In the legal literature, there has been considerable discussion of the difference between appreciating what one is doing and merely knowing it.[26] To the extent that there is any consensus in Canadian jurisprudence, it seems to be that appreciating requires as well the capacity to foresee and measure at least the physical consequences of one's act (though not the emotional consequences, for the victim or others, or the personal consequences, such as apprehension and prosecution).[27] So in the case of a murder, this would mean understanding, at a minimum, that shooting or stabbing or bludgeoning someone is likely to cause their death.

While a successful insanity defence requires lack of capacity to appreciate the nature and quality of one's act, it merely requires lack of capacity to know that the act is wrong. Because appreciating is taken to be more cognitively demanding than mere knowing, this differential formulation suggests a lower bar for satisfying the first branch of the test than for the second. As the Supreme Court would later put it:

> In the ordinary usage of these words it would appear that to appreciate embraces the act of knowing but the converse is not necessarily true. The verb "know" has a positive connotation requiring a bare awareness, the act of receiving information without more. The act of appreciating, on the other hand, is a second stage in a mental process requiring the analysis of knowledge or experience in one manner or another. It is therefore clear on

the plain meaning of the section that Parliament intended that for a person to be insane within the statutory definition, he must be incapable firstly of appreciating in the analytical sense the nature and quality of the act or of knowing in the positive sense that his act was wrong.[28]

At least in principle, therefore, an accused could suffer from "natural imbecility" or a "disease of the mind" that left them capable of understanding what they were doing but rendered them incapable of foreseeing and measuring the consequences of their act. In that case, they might be able to successfully plead insanity.

For the second branch, a successful plea would require that the accused lack the supposedly more basic capacity to know that their act was wrong. But what would this knowledge involve? There has been even more discussion in the courts, and in the legal literature, of the meaning of "wrong" than of the meaning of "appreciate."[29] In particular, should "wrong" be interpreted as "morally wrong" or "legally wrong?" Sir James Fitzjames Stephen, from whose *Draft Code* Section 11 of the 1892 *Criminal Code* was adapted, clearly intended the former.[30] However, during the nineteenth century, the English courts tended to assume the latter.[31]

In the 1920s, this question was unsettled in Canadian law, though there had been some cases that followed the English precedent.[32] It came to be settled by the Supreme Court only much later, in *R. v. Chaulk* (1990):

[I]t is plain to me that the term "wrong" ... must mean more than simply "legally wrong." In considering the capacity of a person to know whether an act is one that he ought or ought not to do, the inquiry cannot terminate with the discovery that the accused knew that the act was contrary to the formal law. A person may well be aware that an act is contrary to law but, by reason of "natural imbecility" or disease of the mind, is at the same time incapable of knowing that the act is morally wrong in the circumstances according to the moral standards of society.[33]

Under this ruling, a mental disorder could provide the accused with a defence, if they lacked the capacity to know *either* that their act was legally wrong *or* that it was morally wrong.

Though the ruling remains definitive, it also appears to conflate two different meanings of "morally wrong." For any given act, such as murder, a perpetrator might lack the capacity to know (a) that it is wrong (something they should not do), or (b) that it is generally regarded as wrong (contrary to the moral standards of society). As every philosophy undergraduate knows, there is a difference between an act being wrong and it being generally thought to be wrong. There is therefore a difference between knowing the former and knowing the latter. American abolitionists in the early nineteenth century knew that slavery was wrong, but they also knew that it was not generally thought to be wrong, especially in the South. By contrast, in Canada in the 1950s, enlightened folk knew that sex between men was not wrong, but they also knew that it was generally thought to be wrong. The two kinds of knowledge will part company whenever common moral standards are wrongheaded or perverse or based merely on tradition or superstition. Furthermore, these two kinds of knowledge presuppose two different kinds of cognitive capacity. To be able to distinguish right from wrong requires the capacity to comprehend and apply moral concepts and moral rules, and to reason to moral conclusions. To determine whether something is generally approved or disapproved in one's society, on the other hand, requires the capacity to acquire knowledge of social facts. It is possible to possess the latter capacity while lacking the former (and possibly vice versa, though that would be more unusual).

The Supreme Court's explication of "morally wrong" is puzzling because it sometimes seems that what the Court had in mind was the moral capacity to distinguish right from wrong:

> The test ... is directed, as emphasized above, at an analysis of the capacity of the accused to reason and to understand the meaning of the terms "right" and "wrong," concepts that demand a moral judgment on the part of every individual in order to be applied in practice. It cannot be determined that an accused does not have the necessary capacity to engage in such moral reasoning simply because he or she does not have the simple ability to retain factual information, for example, the ability to know that a certain act is a crime in the formal sense.[34]

In this passage, the Court contrasts the ability to engage in moral reasoning with the ability to retain factual information. But the information that a certain act is socially disapproved is just as factual as the information that it is a crime. It is odd, therefore, that the Court might identify "morally wrong" with "generally regarded as morally wrong." The Court did, however, have a reason for taking this interpretive line, because it was concerned that in the application of the insanity test, what was morally wrong might be "judged by the personal standards of the offender," which might be at odds with those of society at large.

"The accused," the Court said, "will not benefit from substituting his own moral code for that of society. Instead, he will qualify for an insanity defence only if he is incapable of understanding that the act is wrong *according to the ordinary moral standards of reasonable members of society*."[35]

However, this concern seems misplaced. To benefit from the insanity defence, the accused must first be found to suffer from a serious mental disorder: either a "disease of the mind" or "natural imbecility." Then this disorder must cause an incapacity to distinguish right from wrong. It will therefore not suffice that an offender holds eccentric or idiosyncratic moral convictions; their ability to form any such convictions and reason with them must have either been disordered by psychosis (as it was in M'Naghten's case) or undeveloped due to an intellectual disability.

Fast forward to 2020, and we find that these interpretative issues are still very much with us. On the afternoon of 23 April 2018, a young man named Alek Minassian drove a rented van down a busy street in north Toronto, much of the time on the sidewalk, deliberately targeting pedestrians. In this manner, he killed ten people and injured another sixteen. At his trial in November–December 2020, Minassian raised a "not criminally responsible" defence under the terms of (what is now) Section 16 of the *Criminal Code*, based on his autism spectrum disorder (ASD).[36] That he had this condition was conceded by all concerned, and Ontario Superior Court Justice Anne Malloy agreed that it qualified as a mental disorder within the meaning of Section 16. There was also no question that Minassian knew exactly what he was doing and that it was unlawful. The defence therefore turned on the issue of whether the disorder rendered him incapable of knowing that his act was morally wrong.

Some thirteen closely argued pages of Justice Malloy's reasons for judgment are devoted to the question of what "morally wrong" means in this context. The position she takes, following *Chaulk*, is that "the issue is whether the accused possessed the capacity to know that the act in question was morally wrong *having regard to the everyday standards of the ordinary person*."[37] But that is not all. Following further Supreme Court precedent,[38] Justice Malloy elaborates that more is required than merely the capacity to know intellectually that society would consider the act to be wrong. Additionally, the accused must have "a capacity to rationally evaluate what he is doing and to make a rational choice to do it."[39] This further requirement seems to amount to having the capacity to apply everyday moral standards to the particularities of one's act. This seems even clearer when Justice Malloy restates the requirement: "There must, in addition, be an exercise of a rational choice, recognizing the moral wrongfulness of the act and nevertheless freely choosing to proceed with it."[40] Justice Malloy ultimately concluded that Minassian's ASD did not deprive him of the capacity to know that what he was doing was wrong, nor the capacity to make a free choice to do it regardless, in order to gain notoriety.[41] She therefore convicted him of the murders.

That is one way of analyzing Minassian's state of mind, but it is surely not the only one. If we take seriously Minassian's stated intent of inciting the "incel uprising," then we could as easily say that he knew *intellectually* that his act was "morally wrong having regard to the everyday standards of the ordinary person" but nonetheless believed firmly that it was right by his own superior standards. In that case, he had the capacity to engage in moral reasoning – however distorted it might have been – and to freely act on the conclusion of that reasoning. For a mental disorder defence, it is the capacity that is crucial, not the actual conclusions reached by exercising it. Since Minassian's ASD did not deprive him of this capacity, his insanity defence would still fail.

The final difference between the 1892 *Criminal Code* formulation and the M'Naghten Rules was potentially the most consequential. The two branches of the Rules were disjunctive: the accused must fail to know *either* the nature and quality of the act *or* that it is wrong. However, owing to a "draftsman's error," the *Code* formulation was conjunctive: for a successful defence, it must be shown that the accused lacked the capacity *both* to appreciate the former *and* to know the latter. Where two requirements are specified, it is obviously more difficult to satisfy both than just one of them. For example, to be entitled to a driver's licence, it is more demanding to require that you pass both a written test and a road test than that you pass either one of them. Under the M'Naghten Rules, satisfying either branch of the insanity test would be sufficient for a successful defence, while under the *Code* formulation, satisfying both would be necessary. The "draftsman's error" therefore made it much more difficult to mount a successful defence.

The 1892 provisions concerning the insanity defence were not substantively changed, but only renumbered, in the 1927 consolidation of the *Criminal Code*. They were therefore still in effect at the time of Mike Hack's 1928 trial, including the "draftsman's error." That error played an important role in at least one Canadian murder trial. On 1 March 1895, a twenty-year-old Irish immigrant named Valentine Shortis killed two men and seriously wounded a third in the course of an attempted payroll robbery at the Montreal Cotton Company in Valleyfield, Quebec.[42] He was then charged with two counts of murder and one count of attempted murder. As there were witnesses to the crimes, and as Shortis had freely admitted them, the only issue at his trial in October was his state of mind. In support of a plea of insanity, the defence presented testimony to Shortis's odd and erratic behaviour and his cognitive deficiency by numerous people who knew him well, including both his parents. The court also heard expert testimony by four psychiatrists – or alienists, as they were then known – including Dr. C.K. Clarke, after whom the Clarke Institute of Psychiatry[43] would eventually be named, to (what they called) Shortis's "moral imbecility." The Crown, for its part, presented various rebuttal witnesses, though no expert evidence by alienists.

In his charge to the jury, Justice Michel Mathieu of the Quebec Superior Court repeatedly emphasized the conjunctive nature of the *Criminal Code* insanity test, meaning that for the defence to succeed, the jury would have to find that Shortis lacked the capacity both to appreciate the nature and quality of his act and to know that it was wrong.[44] The defence failed because the jury found that the accused was not insane and convicted him of murder. Shortis was accordingly sentenced to death. After a long and complicated clemency appeal process, which involved no fewer than four Cabinet meetings and a final decision by the governor general himself, the death sentence was commuted to life imprisonment. Shortis remained incarcerated in various institutions until April 1937, when he was given a ticket of leave. He died in Toronto four years later.

Notwithstanding Justice Mathieu's ruling in the Shortis trial, by the 1920s, the dominant tendency in the Canadian courts was to interpret the insanity test in terms of the common law M'Naghten Rules, where the two prongs are plainly disjunctive.[45] The "draftsman's error" did not achieve official judicial notice until an Ontario Court of Appeal case of 1931, at which Chief Justice William Mulock delivered the following judgment:

> This section [s. 19(1) of the 1927 *Code*] is in the very words of sec. 11, subsec. 1, of the *Act entitled the Criminal Code* (1892), and the question is whether the word "and" before the words "of knowing" is to be interpreted literally or as meaning "or." This section is in the exact words of one of the rules in *M'Naghten's case* ... except that it substitutes the word "and" for "or." That this change was a mistake on the part of the draughtsman appears to me obvious. It is a fundamental principle that *mens rea* is an essential element in crime. If absent there is no crime. Here, if the accused did not know that in killing his wife he was doing what was wrong he had no guilty intention and therefore was not guilty of murder, even though he might have appreciated the physical not the moral nature and quality of his act.[46]

This interpretation was adopted by the Saskatchewan Court of Appeal in 1934,[47] and from that time forward, the disjunctive formulation was simply assumed by the Canadian courts, though not formally rectified until the 1954 revision of the *Criminal Code*.

The 1927 *Code* allowed for two different ways in which a finding of insanity on the part of the accused might forestall a conviction. Raising a defence of insanity at trial required establishing that the accused was insane at the time of committing the offence. This was Daniel M'Naghten's situation, and if successful, the defence would result in a finding of not guilty due to insanity. This acquittal would not, however, result in freedom for the accused. We have seen already that M'Naghten spent the rest of his days incarcerated in a mental institution. The 1927 *Code* stipulated that anyone acquitted on grounds of insanity was to be "kept in strict custody in such place and in such manner as to the Court seems fit, until the pleasure of the Lieutenant-Governor is known."[48]

Alternatively, it could be argued that the accused is insane at the time of their trial. According to the 1927 *Code*:

> 967. If at any time after the indictment is found, and before the verdict is given, it appears to the Court that there is sufficient reason to doubt whether the accused is then, on account of insanity, capable of conducting his defence, the Court may direct that an issue shall be tried whether the accused is or is not then, on account of insanity, unfit to take his trial.

In later versions of the *Criminal Code*, the meaning of unfitness to stand trial would be further specified as being "unable on account of mental disorder to conduct a defence at any stage of the proceedings before a verdict is rendered or to instruct counsel to do so, and, in particular, unable on account of mental disorder to (a) understand the nature or object of the proceedings, (b) understand the possible consequences of the proceedings, or (c) communicate with counsel."[49] In the 1927 *Code*, a finding that the accused is unfit to stand trial was to have the same outcome as an acquittal on grounds of insanity: "the accused [is] to be kept in custody till the pleasure of the Lieutenant-Governor of the province shall be known."[50]

Either an application for a declaration of unfitness to stand trial, or a defence of insanity during trial, would be put to the jury to decide. Because of the *Criminal Code* presumption of sanity, the burden of proof to establish insanity would have been on the defence – the opposite of the Crown's burden to establish guilt on the murder charge itself. Again, unlike the criminal charge, the jury would have been required to render its verdict concerning insanity on a balance of probabilities.

The case need not be proved beyond a reasonable doubt. If successful, either strategy would have resulted in a finding of "not guilty by reason of insanity" (nowadays: "not criminally responsible due to mental disorder"). Should this line of defence have succeeded for Hack, then his detention in a mental institution would have lasted until such time (if ever) as he was deemed to be no longer a danger to society. It could quite possibly have lasted for life (as it did for Daniel M'Naghten).

The institution in question would almost certainly have been the Weyburn Mental Hospital, situated about a hundred miles to the south and west of the Pheasant Hills area. When opened in 1921, the hospital became the second such facility in the province, after the Saskatchewan Mental Hospital in North Battleford.[51] Like its predecessor, the Weyburn Hospital was primarily designed as a custodial institution housing two populations of residents: the mentally ill and the mentally defective. However long Hack might have been incarcerated there, his daily life would have been harsh.[52] Though the building was still quite new in 1928, it was falling apart on the inside. Because it had no ventilation system, the air quality was stagnant at best and toxic at worst. The facility was both overcrowded – which meant that violent patients could not be properly segregated from the general population – and understaffed. The problem of understaffing was addressed by requiring all patients to work for up to ten hours a day.

> If they could work, they did. If they were too old to work, they might be placed in the "warehouse," where patients were subjected to custodial care. The refractory patients ... were confined to the basement wards. Here, patients were rarely clothed, frequently restrained, and endured weekly sewer backups that flooded the wards with raw sewage. Throughout the hospital, psychiatric treatment, other than the deceptively named "work therapy," was rare and the structure of the institution was closer to that of a prison than a medical facility.[53]

Given the realities of life at a facility like Weyburn, it was hardly advantageous for an accused to be found unfit to stand trial, or to be acquitted at trial on grounds of insanity, unless the penalty for conviction would be even worse. In Hack's case, however grim an extended stay at the facility might have been, the alternative was definitely worse.

# 6
# "He was German, he was deaf and a little simple"

Mike Hack was the tenth of thirteen children born to Mathias and Dorothea, and it was evident early on that he was different from all his siblings. Mike was a slow learner and did not start school, at grade two level, until 1914, when he was thirteen years old. By the end of that year, he was done with formal schooling and never returned. He was not, however, illiterate; he spoke, read, and wrote both English and German and seemed especially fond of reading his Bible. When he was fifteen, it was time for him to be confirmed in the Lutheran Church. According to one of his fellow confirmation students, Mike was well-behaved and an attentive student, but could not learn the answers to the confirmation questions and was considered "simple-minded." The other children called him "dummy" because he was small and backward. As a result, he became withdrawn, sometimes ill-tempered, and afraid to talk to strangers.[1]

This assessment of simple-mindedness appears to have been shared by the other members of Mike's family. The post-trial affidavits contributed by his mother and his brother Fred, in support of the appeal for clemency, both spoke to his mental condition. Dorothea stated, "During Mike's whole life, we have had trouble with him, and have not considered him to be of normal mentality …"[2] Likewise, Fred stated, "During his whole life, my mother, father, and all my sisters and brothers, and I have considered Mike not to be of normal mentality … We have never considered him to be in his right senses …"[3]

His condition was also common knowledge in the local community. Walter Krahn, the minister of Mike's church, the Missouri Lutheran Church in Neudorf, said in his post-trial affidavit: "From his actions, I have always considered him to be queer, and at times not mentally sound … It is the general impression of the community that [he] has always been queer …"[4]

These assessments, that Mike was "queer,"[5] "not of normal mentality,"[6] and "not in his right senses"[7] run through the statements provided by those in the area who knew him. A petition in support of clemency, signed by more than seventy residents of Neudorf, attested to Mike being "very queer and not of normal mind," "not mentally sound," and "mentally defective."

Mike's mental condition appears to have pushed him to the fringes of his own family. Three of the Hack children died in early childhood and two others died at the ages of fifteen and twenty-five (the latter from the 1918 influenza pandemic). By 1928, all seven of Mike's surviving siblings had married and moved to farms of their own. Only Mike was still living at home with his parents and, after his father died in 1925, with his mother Dorothea. In fact, "living at home" is a bit of an overstatement. Although the family home was his most frequent place of residence, he also tended to move freely about the Pheasant Hills region, staying sometimes with siblings and at other times leaning on the hospitality of anyone who would offer him a meal and a bed.

In his 2012 book *Far from the Tree: Parents, Children, and the Search for Identity*, Andrew Solomon draws a useful distinction between two kinds of identity for children.[8] Vertical identity is constituted by common traits that link a child with parents. In Mike's case, these traits included race, ethnicity, language, religion, socioeconomic status, and occupation – all of them capable of forging strong bonds. This identity can, however, be threatened by equally significant features that serve to distinguish a child from parents. One such feature is disability, to which Solomon devotes one chapter of his book.[9] Disabilities, of course, come in many forms – both physical and mental – and in many degrees of seriousness. In the cases Solomon discusses, parents are struggling to cope with children with multiple severe disabilities, most of whom will never walk, talk, or feed themselves. By contrast, Mike's cognitive impairment was moderate, allowing him to live, in most respects, a relatively normal life. He was, as we might say, disabled but high-functioning. Nonetheless, his condition was sufficient to set him apart from all his other siblings, and to cause his parents, who would have had no previous experience and no social support to fall back on, special problems with his upbringing.

Besides referencing his "queer mentality," the testimonials of his family members also speak to Mike's volatile temperament. His mother Dorothea stated: "if he was crossed, he would act like a baby, or fly into an uncontrollable rage." His brother Fred attested: "at times he was quite mild and easy to get along with, and at other times, he would break into fits of anger and was absolutely uncontrollable." The same behaviour was familiar to local residents who knew him well. Jacob Niebergall stated: "Though apparently being a very mild mannered man, he was subject to work himself up into fury over the very slightest provocation, and when in such fits of anger he seemed to completely lose control of himself, and nobody could do anything with him." Walter Krahn observed: "he had the most uncontrollable temper, and would break out into angry passions over nothing. At other times, he would act like a baby and break into spells of crying, and no one knew just how to take him."

Besides his extreme moods, another theme that appears frequently in these testimonies is Mike's sometimes erratic and seemingly irrational behaviour. In his affidavit, his brother Fred related how, when Mike was living with his sister Katie and her husband Jacob Schick, "[he] quarrelled with them and locked up the door of the room he was living in and would crawl in and out of the window, refusing to eat with them, and saying they stole his food." He added: "My sister also informed me ... that he threatened to kill her baby for this fancied wrong." Fred also told the following story (the same story was related by Mike's mother Dorothea in her affidavit):

> [Mike] would go to almost any ends to obtain anything he might desire, and after obtaining same he would leave it anywhere and with any person, and even make a trade at a very poor bargain to himself; in fact, often giving money, to boot, for something that was practically useless. For example, a year ago last Fall he traded a good car for a poorer one, and eventually traded that and had to pay another man something to boot, then tore the car he received all apart and left the parts at different places.

When Mike's father Mathias died in August 1925, he owned two quarter-sections of land. One of these he left to his wife Dorothea "together with all horses, other stock and all equipment."[10] The other he left to Mike who, at this time, was the only remaining child without a farm of his own. However, according to Jacob Niebergall, the executor of the estate, Mathias shared the family perception that Mike was "not quite right mentally."[11] As he evidently distrusted Mike's ability to manage the farm, in his will, he instructed Niebergall to hold the property for a year and to then convey it only if he was satisfied that Mike "has lived the life of the average good citizen and intends to continue living the life of the average good citizen." Mike did manage to see out the year of good behaviour but, according to Niebergall, "after he obtained [the farm] he reverted to his former self, taking spells of uncontrollable temper, and becoming moody and pettish at times."

Walter Krahn relates his experience in the spring of 1927, when Mike and his mother Dorothea sold both of their farms to Philip Armbruster: "After the deal was all completed and everything arranged as agreed upon, I had considerable trouble with Mike. He would come to me with all his troubles and I would go into the details, explaining everything to him, and he would appear to understand and be quite satisfied with everything, and in a day or so he would come back crying that they were stealing his money and taking his land, whereas, everything was as arranged, and he had his bank book showing that his money was in the bank, and he was told his deed and his contract were also there." Dorothea tells a similar story: "Though at times he appeared to understand everything that was told to him, within a few days time, he might get another idea and I would have a terrible time trying to pacify him, and I never knew just what mood he would be in next."

Both Mike's mother and his brother Fred claim furthermore that he should have been institutionalized. Dorothea stated: "I have always been afraid of him, and wanted him to stay with somebody who would watch over him, as I never considered him in his right senses." Fred added: "At times I have been afraid of him myself, as I never knew when he would have some fancied wrong against me, and my opinion is, that it would be in the best interests of everybody if he were put in some institution where he could do no harm." The signatories to the petition in support of clemency also pleaded that Mike be "committed to a hospital for mentally defectives."

Besides his volatile temperament and erratic behaviour, Mike also acquired a reputation in the community for petty theft. A contemporary tells the following stories:

> Mike's family were very concerned about their son's behavior. They told the story of how Mike's sister's pendant watch, of which she was very proud, disappeared. The parents were certain that Mike had taken it. In an effort to force him to admit his thievery they put his head on a chopping block and threatened him with an upraised axe. Mike, undaunted, refused to admit fault and foiled their attempts. The second story involves several ... bicycles which had been stolen in the Lemberg area ... At the time, Mike was working at the farm of Len and Albert Heaslip's father ... The police suspected Mike – came to the farm and found Mike in his bunkhouse (granary) with several bikes which he had parts interchanged – presumably to hide their identifying marks.[12]

Fred relates a similar story: "He has been in trouble before for stealing a horse and buggy and bicycle, and though the facts and the evidence showed that there was no question but that he took them, he still persisted that he knew nothing about the horses and bicycle, even when they were found in his possession."

The thefts led to trouble with the law. In September 1919, when Mike was eighteen years old, he was charged with the theft of a horse and buggy belonging to William Essel. The horse and buggy had been left outside a store in Neudorf while Essel ran errands. Mike simply drove away with them and was quickly apprehended in possession of the stolen goods. Upon conviction by Judge T.J. Blain, he received a suspended sentence. He was back in court in May 1923 before W.W. King and J.G. Slater, justices of the peace, once again convicted of theft. This time he was assessed a $10 fine, plus costs, and sentenced to two months hard labour in the Regina Jail for both offences. Solomon cites criminal behaviour on the part of a child as another factor inhibiting vertical identity with the parents.[13] Most of the cases he discusses feature crimes much more serious than Mike's petty thefts, though not more serious than the murder he ultimately committed. Mike's various legal troubles, both slight and grave, would have further accentuated his otherness and alienated him even more from his parents and his siblings.

Mike had not one disability but two. Solomon devotes another chapter of his book to the problems encountered by hearing parents with deaf children.[14] In the cases he discusses, the child's deafness is congenital, whereas Mike's deafness was acquired at the age of twenty-one, following a bout of mumps. The difference is important, because by the time he became deaf, Mike had learned to both speak and write (in two languages). However, from the onset of his deafness he lacked an important medium of communication with his parents and his siblings. Neither he nor his family members learned to sign (indeed they had no one to teach them). Besides being able to speak, Mike could read lips a little, but, as evidenced by the investigation of George Edey's murder and the subsequent trial, any complicated communication with others had to be in writing. This barrier would have increased Mike's distance from both family members and local residents and officials. Furthermore, the consequences of his two disabilities appear to have been more than additive: his brother Fred observed that Mike's deafness "seems to have accentuated his queer mentality."[15]

The hypothesis that Mike's cognitive impairment, deafness, and criminality combined to alienate him from his family would serve to explain something that might otherwise seem surprising. Though he was accused of committing the most serious crime, carrying the most serious penalty, there is no record of any of his seven siblings (not even his brother Fred or sister Dora) attending any stage of his trial. The only family member to make an appearance was his mother Dorothea, on the day of the verdict and sentencing. Later, during the appeal for clemency, only Dorothea and Fred contributed affidavits on his behalf. By that time, his other siblings may just have written him off.

Vertical identity, or the lack thereof, is only half of the story for children who have fallen "far from the tree." A ruptured or attenuated vertical identity can be compensated by development of a horizontal identity, which, as Solomon construes it, is constituted by associations with peers who share the child's distinguishing condition(s). These associations can be constructed informally by parents who seek out other families struggling with similar issues, or they can be fostered by special-purpose organizations, such as schools for the deaf or the developmentally delayed. However they are arranged, these horizontal attachments can enable children to socialize without stigma, teach them valuable coping skills (such as signing in the case of deafness), and reassure them that they are not alone with their condition(s). In short, these attachments can enable the child to find a peer group with whom they can build an identity.

None of these arrangements were available to Mike or his family in rural Saskatchewan. There were no social services, no special needs schools, no home visits, no professional support of any kind to help the family deal with a cognitively impaired child, who later also became a hearing-impaired adult, and no identity community where Mike could have had the opportunity to associate with peers who shared either of his disabilities. As a result, he became increasingly isolated from both family and local community and adopted a solitary and nomadic lifestyle. He had previously been capable of keeping a steady job; at one point, he worked for Sid Matthews (brother of Tom, the Duff shopkeeper) for two years. But during the months leading up to the murder, he was usually found roaming the area with his rifle and stopping in for a meal or a bed with any farmer willing to accommodate him. Edey was one such farmer.

Everyone who knew Mike Hack appears to have regarded him as a temperamental, unpredictable, untrustworthy, self-destructive, and sometimes frightening simpleton. Summing up, his younger sister Dora, who knew him as well as anyone, said that "He was German, he was deaf, and a little simple."[16] The picture that forms from all the available evidence is that of a child in a man's body. Alone among his siblings, he never managed to leave the family home to make an independent life for himself. Though he owned farms on two different occasions, he was never able to successfully manage either of them. His father quite evidently doubted that he would ever be able to do so as he left all the necessary farm equipment, including horses, to Hack's mother. Hack entertained fantasies of being an independent farmer – thus his determination to acquire some horses – but they were never more than fantasies. He was full of plans and ideas, but they were usually quickly abandoned in favour of other plans and ideas. As for the other features of his makeup – his uncontrollable bouts of rage and crying, his sometimes erratic behaviour, his petulance and stubbornness, and his habit of taking things he wanted, making no serious attempt to avoid detection, and then denying responsibility for his actions in the face of incontrovertible evidence – they are all the earmarks of a child. In this respect, Hack resembles another childlike itinerant farmhand, this one fictional. The character of Lennie Small, in John Steinbeck's *Of Mice and Men* (1937), is similarly mentally deficient and unable to function on his own. He too kills someone, and he too is executed as a result.

Hack's immaturity manifested itself again in the murder of Edey. Though he made some efforts to conceal his crime, by burying Edey's body in the manure pile, forging receipts for the items he took, and claiming to have helped move Edey to Lorlie, they were pathetic in their ineptitude. No one making a serious attempt to avoid detection for a murder would then drive around the area for days afterward with the dead man's possessions. Though he had been convicted of theft twice before, he seemed to be in a state of denial that he would be caught on this occasion. As Herbert Sampson, the Crown prosecutor, said of Hack, "He is not particularly bright, as one could scarcely say that a bright person would think that he could commit such an offence, under the circumstances ... and get away with it."[17] Someone with the mentality of a child could think that.

Furthermore, Hack's plan to acquire Edey's horses so that he could work the farm he had purchased earlier in the year was completely daft. He had never shown the level of maturity necessary to be an independent farmer, as opposed to a farmhand. He also had no other equipment, because all his father's equipment had been left to his mother and then sold to Philip Armbruster, so the horses alone would have been entirely useless.

Percy Anderson was fully aware of Hack's intellectual disability. In his letter to the minister of justice following Hack's conviction, in which he urged clemency for his client, Anderson stated: "There is no doubt in my mind that [he] is not normal and is not mentally sound." Despite this awareness, Anderson chose not to make an issue of Hack's mental condition at his trial, even though the prosecution expected him to. Sampson anticipated that Anderson would either seek a declaration of unfitness to stand trial or raise a defence of insanity at trial, and he was prepared for both options by having expert witnesses on hand to rebut any testimony to Hack's mental unsoundness. To have any chance of success with either strategy, Anderson would have to interview family members and other local residents prepared to testify to their experience of Hack's mental condition, and find expert witnesses of his own to offer evidence of his cognitive disability. There is no indication that he did either.

Anderson's defence of Hack was underwhelming, to say the least. But how far did it fall below the level of performance expected of defence counsel, especially in a capital case where the client's life is on the line? It is now well established in Canadian law that an accused person enjoys a constitutional right to effective assistance from counsel.[18] For better or worse,[19] in 2000, following the lead of several provincial courts of appeal, the Supreme Court of Canada adopted its approach to ineffectiveness claims from a 1984 decision by the United States Supreme Court.[20] That decision held that in adjudicating such a claim a court must begin with "a strong presumption that counsel's conduct falls within the wide range of reasonable professional assistance."[21] It then continued:

> A convicted defendant's claim that counsel's assistance was so defective as to require reversal of a conviction or death sentence has two components. First, the defendant must show that counsel's performance was deficient. This requires showing that counsel made errors so serious that counsel was not functioning as the "counsel" guaranteed the defendant by the Sixth Amendment. Second, the defendant must show that the deficient performance prejudiced the defense. This requires showing that counsel's errors were so serious as to deprive the defendant of a fair trial, a trial whose result is reliable. Unless a defendant makes both showings, it cannot be said that the conviction or death sentence resulted from a breakdown in the adversary process that renders the result unreliable.[22]

In adopting this approach, the Canadian Court followed the American model in stipulating that "The analysis proceeds upon a strong presumption that counsel's conduct fell within the wide range of reasonable professional assistance. The onus is on the appellant to establish the acts or omissions of counsel that are alleged not to have been the result of reasonable professional judgment."[23] It then proceeded to state that the tests of ineffectiveness "contain a performance component and a prejudice component. For an appeal to succeed, it must be established, first, that counsel's acts or omissions constituted incompetence and second, that a miscarriage of justice resulted."[24] Incompetence, the Court said, was to be determined by a reasonableness standard. As for the requirement of a miscarriage of justice: "In some instances, counsel's performance may have resulted in procedural unfairness. In others, the reliability of the trial's result may have been compromised."[25]

Establishing incompetence in a particular case would involve demonstrating some act or omission that fell below the standards reasonably expected of defence counsel. Among the omissions that may qualify as incompetent is the failure to interview or call a potential defence witness.[26] Anderson failed to interview or call any witnesses. There were many acquaintances and family members who were prepared to testify to Hack's mental unsoundness after his conviction, to try to save him from being hanged, either by submitting affidavits or by signing a petition. It is only reasonable to assume that at least some of them would also have been willing to testify to this effect at a trial where conviction carried with it an automatic death sentence. During preparation of his defence of Hack, Anderson either knew or ought reasonably to have known that these witnesses were available.[27] If he was disinclined to drive the ninety miles from Regina to the Pheasant Hills area to interview them himself, he could have asked William Elliott, his co-counsel on the ground there, to do it for him. In addition to this testimony by private citizens, expert evidence by alienists would also be needed. In this case, because the required witnesses were not ready to hand and willing to testify, it would have been Anderson's responsibility to seek them out and engage their services. Failure to do so was a further indication of negligence. The performance component of the ineffectiveness tests would therefore appear to be satisfied.[28]

Turning to the prejudice component, the US Court held that a claimant must establish "a reasonable probability that, but for counsel's unprofessional errors, the result of the proceeding would have been different. A reasonable probability is a probability sufficient to undermine confidence in the outcome ..."[29] In general, Canadian appeal courts have tended to settle the question of prejudice by asking whether trial counsel's incompetence undermined the reliability of the verdict.[30] In that case, the question becomes whether making an issue of Hack's mental condition, with testimony from the appropriate witnesses, might have had a reasonable probability of leading to an outcome other than his conviction: either a finding of unfitness to stand trial or an acquittal on grounds of insanity.

The first step would have been to establish that Hack suffered from either "natural imbecility" or a "disease of the mind." There was no evidence to suggest that Hack was psychotic or otherwise delusional

– at least no reliable evidence. Before his trial, Hack was examined on 22 July, and again on 30 September, by Dr. Alexander Douglas Campbell, assistant superintendent (soon to become superintendent) of the Weyburn Mental Hospital. Campbell reported that he noticed something different about Hack on the second occasion: "The difference apparently being that some person had been speaking to the accused in the interval, as a result of which the accused was somewhat primed for the examination and then said he heard strange noises, etc., which state of affairs did not exist at the time of the first examination."[31] It seems likely that the person in question was either Anderson or Elliott, in which case we can surmise that they thought an effective insanity defence would require evidence of delusions. Hack's "strange noises" seem to have been coached and feigned for the purpose of the examination, and there is nothing in what we know of his life to suggest that he had ever previously experienced them.

If it could not be established that Hack was psychotic, then the case would have to be made on the basis of "natural imbecility." If he did have an intellectual disability, as appears to be the case, it is no easy matter to determine just how subnormal his intelligence was. While he was examined on those two occasions by Dr. Campbell, there is no record that he was ever administered the Binet–Simon test. Dr. Campbell did commonly use IQ testing as a tool to classify resident patients at the Weyburn Hospital, but because parts of the test are oral, he may have felt that Hack's deafness precluded testing in his case. Had a test been administered, it would very likely have resulted in a low score, due to both the subject's hearing disability and his lack of formal schooling. Without a test result to rely on, Dr. Campbell could only report, more vaguely, that Hack was "not of a particularly bright type,"[32] that is, that he suffered from some undetermined degree of cognitive deficiency. Had Dr. Campbell elected to test Hack, and had the test results assigned him to one of the then-recognized three categories of feeble-mindedness, that clinical result would have enormously aided Anderson in making the case that Hack suffered from "natural imbecility."

In the absence of a more helpful clinical opinion from Dr. Campbell, Anderson would have had to engage the services of one or more alienists willing to examine Hack, subject him to the requisite IQ testing, and rebut the evidence of the medical experts – as well as Dr. Campbell, Dr. Oswald E. Rothwell of the Regina Jail – that had been lined up to testify on behalf of the Crown. Alternatively, if requested by defence counsel, Justice Maclean could himself have ordered a psychiatric assessment of Hack. Anderson could also have asked family members and neighbours to come forward to testify to their experience of Hack's "queer" personality and behaviour. Because Hack was a well-known figure in the Pheasant Hills area, some of the jurors may also have had similar experience in their interactions with him. If he had elected to make an issue of Hack's mental condition, Anderson would also have had a reason to put his client on the stand. Had all of this evidence – expert and otherwise – been presented in court, a lawyer of Anderson's skill and experience should have had a very good chance of convincing the jury of Hack's "natural imbecility."

But he would then have had a decision to make about how to use this result to his client's best advantage. Since Hack's intellectual disability was lifelong, he was equally afflicted by it at the time of the offence in May and of the trial in October. Anderson therefore could have argued either that Hack should be found not guilty of the offence by reason of insanity or that he was unfit to stand trial.

If Anderson had elected the former route, then he would have had to show that Hack's cognitive impairment deprived him of the capacity either to appreciate the nature and quality of his act or to know that it was wrong. There seems little doubt that Hack was aware that striking Edey forcefully six times on the head with a blunt instrument was certain to cause him at least grievous injury if not death. Whether he knew that killing Edey was wrong is a more complicated matter.

Much would have depended on how Justice Maclean chose to interpret this branch of the insanity test and how he would have instructed the jury. Perhaps he would have taken "wrong" to mean "legally wrong," as the English courts tended to do, and as was done in the 1882 trial of Michael Lee, who was charged with the brutal axe murder of eighteen-year-old Maggie Howie in Napanee, Ontario.[33] Lee and Howie had been engaged but she had broken off the engagement when she discovered he had a mistress. There was no doubt that Lee had committed the act, so the only question at trial was of his sanity. Two respected alienists testified for the defence: Dr. W.G. Metcalfe, the medical director of the Kingston Asylum for the Insane, and Dr. Daniel Clark, medical superintendent of the Queen Street Lunatic Asylum in Toronto. Both found that Lee was suffering from "acute dementia." In his charge to the jury, Chief Justice Wilson said that the question was whether Lee's mental condition rendered him incapable of knowing that his act was contrary to law. After two and a half hours of deliberation, the jury returned a verdict of guilty and stated that, in this sense, he did know the difference between right and wrong. When his mental condition became worse, his sentence was commuted, and he spent the rest of his life in Kingston Penitentiary.

If Maclean had elected the same interpretation of "wrong," it would have been difficult for Anderson to convince the jury that Hack lacked the capacity to understand that killing Edey was unlawful. Hack had previous experience of being prosecuted for theft, so he would have expected that, if apprehended, he would be prosecuted again, at least for theft if not for murder. He therefore took steps to avoid apprehension, by concealing Edey's body, by forging receipts for his goods, and by concocting the story that Edey had moved to Lorlie.

Alternatively, the trial judge might have been prescient enough to anticipate the Supreme Court and interpret knowing that killing Edey was wrong as knowing that it would be generally condemned by the local community, or the wider Canadian society. These same steps to conceal the crime could also constitute evidence that Hack knew intellectually that his act was wrong in this sense. Even a child is capable of figuring out what family members and neighbours are likely to think about murder.

But suppose instead that Justice Maclean had interpreted "morally wrong" in the plain meaning of the phrase, where knowing that killing Edey was wrong would require Hack to understand that it was something he should not do. In that case, the issue would have been whether his cognitive disability had stunted or distorted his capacity to comprehend and internalize moral norms and to operationalize those norms in his own actions. Here Anderson might have had much better prospects of success. As Hack's brother Fred said, (Mike) "would go to almost any ends to obtain anything he might desire." This pattern of behaviour would be explainable if Hack's cognitive impairment left him with the mentality of a child. Young children often see nothing wrong with taking things that belong to other children and may regard the children who own those things as mere obstacles in their way. As Hack saw it, he needed horses to be able to work the farm he had purchased, Edey owned the best horses in the area, and therefore, he had to have those horses. As he could not afford to buy them, he would obtain them by another means. Edey was merely an obstacle in the way.

It is one thing to speculate that Hack's "natural imbecility" might have deprived him of the capacity an adult would have to know that it was wrong of him to kill Edey. It would be quite another for Anderson to convince a jury of this. He would not have been encouraged had he been familiar with the recent history of such attempts. As we have seen, insanity defences failed for both Valentine Shortis and Michael Lee. More recent, and more pertinent, were two cases that occurred just six years before Hack's trial.

In March 1922, twenty-year-old Bennie Swim was charged with the murder of his cousin, Olive Swim Trenholm, and her husband, Harvey Trenholm, in the small town of Benton Ridge, New Brunswick.[34] For about a year, Bennie had been living with Olive Swim (as she then was) and her father, during which time Bennie and Olive had developed a conjugal relationship. Bennie had hoped to formalize this relationship through marriage, but Olive had rejected him and instead married Harvey Trenholm. The couple had been married for less than two weeks when Bennie turned up at their home, intending to convince Olive to leave her husband. Instead, he shot both of them. He then fled into the surrounding woods where he attempted to kill himself by shooting himself in the head. He was quickly apprehended by the police.

As Swim had readily confessed to the crimes, the only available defence at trial was insanity. His defence counsel, Frederick Charles Squires, attempted to adduce evidence showing that Swim's "natural imbecility" was hereditary. To this effect, he called no expert witnesses, relying instead on the testimony of members of Swim's family, including both of his parents. He did not call Swim himself to the stand. The family members testified that since he had been a boy Swim had experienced "spells" (which appear to have been epileptic seizures) after which he acted "kind of dumb." On this issue, the Crown called no witnesses of its own, relying instead on cross-examination of the defence witnesses.

In his charge to the jury, Chief Justice McKeown was openly sceptical of the insanity defence, pointing out that Swim had planned for the possibility of killing Olive and Harvey by purchasing a revolver before coming to their house. The jury returned a verdict of guilty. When his appeal for clemency was denied, Bennie Swim was hanged on 6 October.[35]

Bennie Swim's case was in some respects similar to that of Fred Baldwin, who in May 1922 was charged with the murder of Robert Molton, a homestead farmer near the border between Ontario and Minnesota, for whom Baldwin was working.[36] Baldwin took room and board with the Molton family, which included a seventeen-year-old daughter named Gladys, with whom Baldwin carried on a clandestine relationship. Baldwin was alleged to have shot Molton out of concern that he would stand in the way of their marriage.

Because the evidence against Baldwin was overwhelming, including his own confession, the only defence raised on his behalf at his November trial was insanity. His defence counsel, Daniel Richmond Byers, argued that Baldwin suffered from "natural imbecility," which caused him to be incapable of knowing that his act of killing Molton was wrong. Evidence was provided by Baldwin's mother of his poor performance in school, which he left at the age of thirteen. Baldwin had enlisted in the army at the age of twenty-eight but had been denied overseas service due to "mental deficiency." Under direct examination by his counsel, Baldwin "was unable to answer what was the capital of Canada, whom we had fought in the war, the colonel of his regiment, or the year of his own birth."[37]

Medical evidence concerning Baldwin's mental condition was provided by Dr. Linden Y. McIntosh, who was a general practitioner, not an alienist. Based on two examinations of Baldwin, McIntosh classified him as a "low grade moron" but not quite an imbecile. McIntosh's testimony was contradicted for the Crown by Dr. James A. Crozier, the surgeon in the Port Arthur Jail, who had been in frequent contact with Baldwin. Crozier declared Baldwin to be "of average intelligence, although not very well educated."[38] The final expert testimony was given by another general practitioner, Dr. Charles J. Johnston, who was unable to conclude that Baldwin was an imbecile.

As for whether Baldwin was capable of knowing that his act was wrong, he himself testified that he did not realize it at the time of the offence but "figured it out after I shot him."[39] This testimony was supported by the fact that immediately after shooting Molton, Baldwin made no attempt to conceal the murder weapon and, only after telling the women in the Molton household what he had done, returned to the scene of the crime and hid the rifle in the nearby creek.

Justice Mowat's charge to the jury was exceedingly hostile to the testimony supporting Baldwin's insanity defence. Unsurprisingly, the jury returned a verdict of guilty after only forty minutes of deliberation, and Baldwin was automatically sentenced to death. An appeal for commutation of the sentence was denied by Cabinet, and Baldwin was duly hanged, by Arthur Ellis, on 15 January 1923, almost exactly six years before Mike Hack would meet the same fate at the hands of the same man.

Between 1920 and 1950, 1443 charges of murder were laid in Canada.[40] Of this total, 173 accused (12 per cent) were found unfit to stand trial. There is no record of the fraction of the 1443 cases in which an unfitness application was filed, but it certainly would not have been all of them. The success rate for such applications must therefore have been considerably higher than 12 per cent. Of the 1270 charges that did go to trial, 692 (54 per cent) resulted in acquittals. There appears to be no record of the proportion of those acquittals that were on grounds of insanity, but anecdotal evidence would suggest that it was quite low. In that case, the statistical evidence strongly suggests that the better option for Anderson would have been to apply for a declaration of unfitness for his client. It would also have been the simpler. As noted earlier, the issue to be put to the jury would have been whether, on account of his mental condition, Hack was incapable of conducting his defence. Anderson himself was in no doubt on this point. In his letter to the minister of justice following Hack's conviction, in which he urged commutation of the death sentence, he offered the following observation about his client:

> When I first had anything to do with him I was impressed with the absolute lack of appreciation of the severity of the crime with which he was charged. This lack of appreciation seemed to continue during the trial, and even after he was found guilty. I do not think it was callousness on his part but a low order of mentality which did not duly appreciate what was transpiring.[41]

Nowadays, sophisticated tools have been developed to determine the fitness of an accused to stand trial, such as the MacArthur Competence Assessment Tool – Criminal Adjudication (MacCat-CA), which employs structured interviews to assess three competence-related abilities: understanding (the ability to comprehend general information related to the law and criminal processes), reasoning (the ability to discern the potential legal relevance of information, and to reason about specific choices that may confront a defendant in the course of a trial), and appreciation (awareness of the meaning and consequences of the proceedings in one's own case).[42] According to his defence counsel, Hack was deficient in all three, but especially in the last two. In 1928, however, the only available tools were general-purpose IQ tests, and Hack was never tested.

The ability of the accused to follow and comprehend what was happening in his trial was compromised by his deafness as well as his cognitive disability. There is evidence that deaf persons face special risks at every stage of the criminal justice process,[43] especially when facing murder charges.[44] The risks are particularly acute when the accused fits the profile of what has come to be known as primitive personality disorder (PPD). The diagnostic criteria for PPD require that at least three of the following conditions be satisfied:

1. Little or no knowledge of sign language.
2. Functional illiteracy (a reading grade level below three).
3. A history of little or no formal education.

4. Pervasive cognitive deprivation, involving little or no ability to manage normal life functions, such as paying bills, holding a job, or planning a budget.
5. A performance IQ of 70 or lower.

Hack fully checked off some of these items and partially checked off others. He knew no sign language and had limited ability at speechreading, which meant that all communication had to be in writing. He had only limited formal education, at the grade two level. However, by the time he became deaf, at the age of 21, he had learned to both read and write; consequently, he was not functionally illiterate. He did have a cognitive impairment, but he seemed to be able to handle many of the tasks of daily life, including maintaining a bank account and even buying a farm. Because his IQ was never tested, we cannot be certain of its exact level; however, in light of Dr. Campbell's assessment that he was "not of a particularly bright type," we may assume that he would have tested some distance below normal.

Because Hack could not hear any of the testimony at his trial, he had to read it in transcription. There is no doubt of his ability to read English, but whether he understood what he was reading in this particular context is another matter. According to Herbert Sampson, the Crown prosecutor, despite Hack's deafness "he seemed to have some knowledge of what each particular witness was testifying in the case."[45] Sampson had no basis for this opinion except his observation of Hack in the prisoner's box. Justice Maclean offered a similar report: "He appeared to be of average intelligence, reasonably astute, read all the evidence, and conferred with his counsel frequently on matters appearing in the evidence. This of course is from my observation during the trial."[46] As conferences between counsel and the accused are confidential, the trial judge had no basis for his assumption that Hack's conversations with Anderson (which would have had to be in writing) concerned "matters appearing in the evidence." According to a contemporary newspaper account of the second day of the trial, Hack "sat motionless through the progress of the case today as he did yesterday apparently oblivious to all about him. Leaning on the right rail of the prisoner's box he gave verbal answers to his lawyers ... as they scribbled questions at intervals."[47]

It would be completely unwarranted to conclude from any of these observations of Hack's conduct in the courtroom that he had any idea at all of what was happening in his trial. Only Anderson's input speaks to this issue, and it is uncompromising: his client's intellectual disability, compounded by his deafness, meant that he could not "duly appreciate what was transpiring" during the trial. Additionally, we have this observation from William Elliott, who visited the convicted man in jail in December, after his conviction and when he was awaiting execution: "he does not seem to have any adequate appreciation of his position whatsoever and a normal minded man could hardly take the view of his position that he does."[48] In light of these reports, it seems very likely that Hack satisfied the later *Criminal Code* criteria of unfitness, by virtue of his inability to (a) understand the nature or object of the proceedings, (b) understand the possible consequences of the proceedings, and (c) communicate with counsel.

It therefore appears that an application for a declaration of unfitness to stand trial would have had the greater likelihood of success. Seeking an acquittal on grounds of insanity would have been both more complicated and more susceptible to rebuttal by the Crown. Whichever path Anderson elected to pursue, the question would have been put to the jury, to be decided on a balance of probabilities. While it is impossible to be certain how the jury might have decided, it is clear that either strategy would have had a much better chance of success than Anderson's actual "defence" of Hack, which consisted solely in challenging the factual evidence that – however circumstantial it might have been – clearly connected the accused to the crime.

Without evidence of his mental condition before the court, Hack stood no chance of avoiding conviction. Had Anderson succeeded with an application for a declaration of unfitness, then there would have been no trial verdict. Had he succeeded instead with an insanity defence, then there would have been no conviction. But even in the worst case, in which both strategies failed, evidence of Hack's intellectual disability would have been on the record, thereby increasing the likelihood of either the trial judge or the jury recommending mercy in his case and providing a much stronger argument for Anderson to seek commutation of Hack's death sentence.

The jury in Hack's murder trial was never presented with evidence of his mental condition. It was therefore never given the option of determining whether, on account of his "natural imbecility," he was unfit to stand trial for the murder of Edey, or, having stood trial, should be acquitted on grounds of insanity. Anderson's failure to interview or call the necessary witnesses satisfies the competence component of the tests for ineffective assistance of counsel. Unlike classic cases of wrongful conviction, like Guy Paul Morin's, the evidence that the jury never got to hear would not have exonerated Hack, as it would not have established his factual innocence. But the fact remains that the missing evidence could well have had a material effect on the outcome of the trial. All that is required for the prejudice component to be satisfied is "a reasonable probability that, but for counsel's unprofessional errors, the result of the proceeding would have been different." The courts have not defined the threshold level of probability that would qualify as "reasonable" (50 per cent chance of success? 25 per cent?), but the likelihood of a successful outcome for Hack, especially from an application for a declaration of unfitness, was certainly well above zero. If that is sufficient to render the jury verdict unreliable, as it would seem to be, then Anderson's defence of his client would qualify as ineffective assistance of counsel and the outcome of the trial would constitute a wrongful conviction and a miscarriage of justice.

In 1928, a person convicted of murder had two legal routes available to avoid execution. One was to initiate an appeal to a provincial appellate court, which was the route taken for most murder convictions. The appeal to a higher court could be of the verdict only, as the death penalty was mandatory upon conviction and could be reduced only by the federal Cabinet. The appeal was of right on a question of law and with leave of the appellate court on a mixed question of law and fact or any other ground.[49] If the appellate court granted the appeal, it then had the power to either quash the conviction or to order a new trial.[50]

Anderson had considerable experience arguing appeals on behalf of criminal defendants. There was in this case no claim to a mistake of law because Anderson seemed to have no objection to Justice Maclean's handling of the trial, including his charge to the jury. Even if the judge's summation of the facts in that charge was somewhat prejudicial to the accused – and it is far from clear that it was – adducing this fault would not have succeeded as a ground of appeal unless it could be shown that, absent the fault, the jury would not have reached the same conclusion.[51] The jury's verdict, however, was entirely reasonable on the basis of the evidence adduced at trial, and there is no reason to think that a fairer charge by Justice Maclean would have led to a different outcome.

Under the terms of the 1927 *Criminal Code*, there was a further ground for a court of appeal to overturn a conviction: a miscarriage of justice at trial.[52] In Hack's case, the basis of an appeal on this ground would have had to be that there was additional evidence – of the mental condition of the accused – that was not heard at trial and that, if heard, could have had a material effect on the verdict. It is far from clear that such an appeal would have succeeded. It is now well established that ineffective assistance of counsel can serve as the ground for an appeal,[53] but there appears to have been no precedent for appealing a murder conviction on this ground prior to 1928.

In any case, the question is academic. Anderson was responsible for the missing material evidence, and he was never likely to appeal the verdict on the ground of his own incompetent defence. As far as can be ascertained, Anderson was in complete control of Hack's defence, both during the trial and thereafter, with little direction either from William Elliott or the Hack family. He would certainly have been getting no direction from his client; as we have seen, Anderson was fully cognizant of Hack's inability to instruct counsel due to his "low order of mentality which did not duly appreciate what was transpiring" at his trial. Anderson appears to have been typical of his time in subscribing to what G. Arthur Martin would later call the "lawyer control" model of the function of defence counsel, on which counsel is to have unfettered discretion over the conduct of the defence.[54] Anderson was exercising this discretion in deciding not to call any defence witnesses at Hack's trial and, in particular, in deciding not to base the defence on Hack's "natural imbecility." He would be exercising the same discretion in deciding not to appeal the trial verdict.

The other route available for avoiding the execution of a convicted murderer was an application to the federal Cabinet for clemency. The best outcome of this application would have been commutation of Hack's death sentence. The clemency process also had the potential to yield the same outcome as a successful appeal of the conviction, namely, the order of a new trial with new evidence. Under the terms of the 1927 *Code*,[55] once an application for clemency was made, the minister of justice had the authority to order a new trial should he come to doubt whether the applicant should have been convicted.[56] One reason for such doubt would be that the clemency process had turned up additional pertinent evidence that was not heard at trial.

Whatever outcome Anderson hoped for from the clemency application, one thing was already quite clear: he had failed his client at the trial stage. His ineffective assistance was just the kind of serious defect in the trial that would render its outcome a wrongful conviction and a miscarriage of justice. Carolyn Strange notes that it was the practice of many judges in capital cases to utter the phrase "you have been ably defended" when preparing to pass sentence following conviction.[57] This phrase was conspicuously absent from Justice Maclean's sentencing of Hack.

This judgment concerning Anderson's performance might seem – or might be – somewhat anachronistic. Hack's conviction occurred in 1928, and the Supreme Court tests of ineffective assistance of counsel were only developed decades later. One might wonder whether there is any point in applying the standards of the present day to the performance of defence counsel nearly a century ago.

Whether there is such a point depends on the question we are attempting to answer. If the question is whether an appeal of Hack's conviction, on the ground of ineffective assistance, might have succeeded at the time, then we must answer that by reference to the standards and precedents of the time. In that case, it seems very likely that any such appeal would have failed. But there is another question we can, and should, be asking: whether Hack received a fair trial. This second question is not the same as the first. Appeals of Steven Truscott's and Guy Paul Morin's convictions failed at the time of their trials, but that did not prevent much later acknowledgment, as the result of official inquiries, that their convictions were wrongful. Likewise, when we judge slavery or the residential school system to have been unjust, we are not applying the standards of their day, which would have exonerated them. Instead, we are using our current standards of justice to contend that these practices always were unjust. In exactly the same way, we can now conclude that Hack's conviction was a miscarriage of justice, though it might not have been regarded as such in its time.

Anderson's defence of Hack was so inept that it is tempting to think that he never seriously intended to try to get his client acquitted by contesting the evidence adduced at trial.[58] He may have quickly come to the conclusion that Hack was a dangerous simpleton who would never get his life together and who, if allowed to go free, would always be liable to reoffend. Anderson may have thought that he did not have enough evidence to mount an effective insanity defence – in which case Hack would have been institutionalized – but did have enough to secure commutation of his sentence upon conviction – in which case he would still be institutionalized. If this conjecture is correct, then Anderson elected to take a terrible gamble with his client's life, one that he would ultimately lose.

# 7
# The Royal Prerogative of Mercy

As soon as the trial verdict was in, on 5 October, "The accused was asked if he desired to say anything, and his counsel, Mr. Anderson, KC, spoke on his behalf intimating that an appeal would be made to the minister of justice with respect to the mental soundness of the accused, and asked that reasonable time might be given for this purpose."[1]

The royal prerogative of mercy is the residue of the absolute power once held by the British monarch to set aside, or provide alternatives to, death sentences imposed by the courts of the land. The 1927 *Criminal Code*, which imposed a mandatory death penalty for murder, provided that the royal prerogative could revise or overturn any sentence dictated by statute, including sentence of death.[2] The prerogative therefore made room for the exercise of executive discretion on the matter of sentencing for murder cases, where the judiciary had none. That the prerogative was intended as a means of heading off injustices that might result from the inflexibility of the mandatory penalty was clearly understood during the period when capital punishment was in force. In 1953, the then minister of justice, Stuart Garson, appointed a Joint Committee of the Senate and House of Commons to look into capital punishment, among other matters. In its *Report on Capital Punishment*, tabled in June 1956, the Committee affirmed that "the exercise of the prerogative of mercy is a necessary and indispensable feature of the mandatory sentence of capital punishment for murder and ... by its use, the severity of the punishment can be mitigated in appropriate cases."[3]

In this era of constitutional monarchies, the prerogative is still officially exercised by the sovereign or the sovereign's representative: in Canada, at least in criminal cases, by the governor general in council. But the real decision is made by the federal Cabinet (since criminal law falls under federal jurisdiction). Before the 1961 law reform, which introduced a category of non-capital murder, Cabinet review of capital cases was automatic. Nor was clemency for convicted murderers merely a faint hope. Between Confederation and 1976, when the death penalty was abolished, some 1,533 death sentences were imposed by Canadian trial courts.[4] Of these, 705 actually resulted in hangings, while 619 were commuted. The remaining 209 cases were resolved in other ways, such as appeal leading to acquittal, appeal leading to new trial and acquittal, appeal leading to new trial on a lesser offence, death in jail prior to execution, suicide in jail. Someone convicted of murder, therefore, had about a 40 per cent chance of being granted clemency. However, the probability of a successful application varied considerably decade by decade during this lengthy period. During the 1920s, the sentence was commuted in 43 per cent of all applications, while during the 1930s, that figure fell to 25 per cent.[5] From 1963, all death sentences were routinely commuted by Cabinet.

By the 1920s, the Cabinet review procedure had settled into a routine.[6] Upon receiving notice of a murder conviction, the Remission Service of the Justice Department began the process of collecting all the relevant documents: trial transcript, exhibits entered as evidence, fingerprints and photographs of the accused, prior convictions of the accused (if any), report of the trial judge, police reports, psychiatric reports (if any), representations on behalf of the accused, and so on. Following a review of these materials, the chief clerk of the Remission Service prepared a memorandum outlining (what they considered) the salient facts of the case and making a recommendation for or against clemency. This memorandum was then presented to Cabinet by the minister of justice (or the solicitor-general, if there was one in Cabinet). In most cases, its recommendation became the decision of Cabinet, which was then rubber-stamped by the governor general. Despite the official roles in the review process for the minister, for Cabinet, and for the governor general, *de facto* the ultimate decision concerning clemency was effectively determined by a bureaucrat – the chief clerk – who in turn relied heavily on the report of the trial judge.[7] The chief clerk in place at the time of Mike Hack's review was Michael F. Gallagher, who held that position from 1924 to 1952 and therefore presided over hundreds of capital cases.

The review process got underway on 6 October, the day after the conclusion of the trial, when Thomas Cromie, the court reporter, sent a copy of the trial transcript to the secretary of state in Ottawa (along with his bill in the amount of $121.95). On 5 November, RCMP headquarters in Ottawa forwarded numerous further items to Gallagher:

copies of Corporal Metcalfe's crime reports, Hack's photograph and fingerprints, and a record of his prior conviction for theft in 1923 (which inexplicably omitted his earlier conviction for theft in 1919). Accompanying the photograph was Hack's personal information: his date and place of birth (the latter given mistakenly as Germany) and his occupation (listed as "farmer," though "farm labourer" or "farmhand" would have been more accurate). Hack was recorded as being five feet seven inches in height and weighing 155 pounds, with a dark complexion, black hair, and dark grey eyes. Under "distinctive marks and peculiarities," the report noted "broken collarbone, left side; both little fingers crooked; scar on end left ring finger; scar on left wrist." The face in the photograph features a prominent nose and a neutral expression that could be read equally well as contemplative or as uncomprehending.

Meanwhile, on 1 November, Percy Anderson made formal application for commutation of the death penalty in a letter to Ernest Lapointe, the minister of justice, in which he made clear what he considered to be the strongest ground for clemency:

> There can be no doubt that Mike Hack was not normal. He was under observation by Dr. Campbell of the Weyburn Mental Hospital, but owing to the fact that he was deaf and everything had to be written on paper, it is rather a difficult case to have much to go on …
>
> I am not just sure what the procedure is in a case of this kind, but I understand that the Department prefers to communicate direct both with the trial judge and with the observing physician.
>
> I am sending material, chiefly affidavits by people who have known him, to shew that he was not normal. I am not familiar with the proceedure [sic], and, therefore, if there is anything that I should provide you, would you be kind enough to indicate the same to me and it will afford me pleasure to do so.

The deputy minister replied on 7 November:

> In response to your query I may say that any representations you may care to submit in support of your petition for clemency should be made in writing, and forwarded as early as possible. When received, they will be attached to the record which will, in due course, be submitted to His Excellency the Governor General in Council.
>
> I may add that if, consequent upon any material you may submit, any enquiries are deemed to be necessary by this Department, such will be instituted in due course.

Anderson finally submitted those "representations" about six weeks later, on 15 December, which consisted of letters from Anderson himself and co-counsel William Elliott, plus affidavits from Dorothea and Fred Hack, Jacob Niebergall, Philip Armbruster, and Walter Krahn. Anderson also noted that a petition was currently circulating in the area. In his letter, he stated:

> I have enquired from people who reside in the District where he lives and they are all of the same opinion that since a child he has not been of sound mind at all but has always acted in a very queer way ...
>
> The general impression in the country where he lives is that it would be a dangerous thing to let this man loose and that he should be put in some place where he can do no harm, but that hanging is hardly the proper remedy for a man in his mental condition.

Elliott made essentially the same point: "It has been the general opinion of the community that Mike was always queer, and he has always been looked upon as such. It is also the general opinion of the community that a man in his mental condition should not be hung."

The affidavits reinforced the same themes:

*Dorothea Hack:*

> ... during Mike's whole life we have had trouble with him, and have not considered him to be of normal mentality.
>
> ... we have had to watch him, as he was very moody, and would fly into uncontrollable anger ...
>
> ... I have always been afraid of him, and wanted him to stay with somebody who would watch over him, as I never considered him in his right senses.
>
> ... if he was crossed, he would act like a baby, or fly into an uncontrollable rage.
>
> ... I feel that he should be put in some institution where he could not do any harm.

*Fred Hack:*

> ... during his whole life, my mother, father and my sisters and brothers, and I have considered Mike not to be of normal mentality ...
>
> ... we have never considered him to be in his right senses, and at times I have been afraid of him myself, as I never knew when he would have some fancied wrong against me, and my opinion is, that it would be in

the best interests of everybody if he were put in some institution where he could do no harm.

*Jacob Niebergall*:

... I myself and all others who knew [Mike] considered him not to be of normal mentality.

*Philip Armbruster*:

... I always considered Mike queer, and not in his right senses ...

... Though apparently being a very mild mannered man, he was subject to work himself up into fury over the very slightest provocation, and when in such fits of anger he seemed to completely lose control of himself and nobody could do anything with him.

... at different times all of us who knew him well considered him not to be in his right senses and considered it was not safe for him to be at large.

*Walter Krahn*:

... from his actions I have always considered [Mike] to be queer, and at times not mentally sound, as he had the most uncontrollable temper, and would break out into angry passions over nothing. At other times he would act like a baby and break into spells of crying, and no one knew just how to take him.

... it is the general impression of the community that the said Mike Hack has always been queer, and that hanging would not be a fit punishment for him, and I am of the opinion that it would be better to place him in some institution where he could do no harm.

While these various materials were being collected and submitted, Hack received a slight reprieve of his execution. On 10 November, Donald Maclean issued an order postponing the hanging from 9 January to 18 January, due to unavailability of an experienced hangman on the earlier date.

Meanwhile, the Remission Service was attempting to extract a report from the trial judge, who seemed to have little understanding of what was expected of him. The first contact with Justice Maclean was a telegram on 14 November from Thomas Mulvey, under secretary of state:

In view of accumulation of capital cases which will require early consideration by Minister of Justice will you be good enough to inform me when your report on Capital Case of Mike Hack may be forwarded to this Department as well as any documentary exhibits which you may think are needed in connection with the case.

The trial judge replied on the following day, also by telegram, saying that on 6 October – the day after the conclusion of the trial – he had forwarded all of the evidence, plus his charge to the jury, and intended this to constitute his report, saying that "there is really nothing that I can add to what was indicated by me in the charge to the jury." He concluded, "In any event, whether requested or not, the exhibits in the case in my opinion would not be of any assistance to you. This is my report and am confirming it by letter," which he did on the following day.

On 19 November, Mulvey forwarded Justice Maclean's response to the deputy minister of justice. The Remission Service was far from satisfied with it. On 22 November, Gallagher sent a memorandum to Lapointe, indicating that the trial judge needed to be brought up to speed on what was expected of him and suggesting that the minister might want to direct his attention to the sections of the *Criminal Code* dealing with the trial judge's report and perhaps also forward to him, for his edification, a sample report by another judge in a previous case. Gallagher went on:

> You might also wish to forward to His Lordship copy of a formal notification of the decision of His Excellency the Governor General in Council in a capital case, which indicates that the report of the trial Judge is an extremely important document in the procedure followed.
>
> I may say that to my knowledge very few of those connected with the administration of Justice realize what a task the appeal for clemency, in each capital case, imposes upon the Minister of Justice – how nerve-racking the proceedings, and how short the time allowed for each and every necessary step.

On the following day, Lapointe forwarded the memo to Justice Maclean, adding "as I have personally to peruse all of the material in these capital cases, and to explain them in detail to my colleagues in Council, I know from personal experience that the detailed report of the trial Judge, covering the circumstances relating to the commission of the crime, as adduced in evidence, together with any other information which may be deemed helpful, is of most invaluable assistance."

This tutorial in proper procedure finally galvanized the trial judge into action. After expressing gratitude for the helpful materials that had been sent to him, and explaining that he had not realized that it would be appropriate for him to express an opinion on the question of commutation, he finally sent his report to Ottawa on 5 December. In it, he reviewed the crime, the police investigation, and the evidence supporting conviction, concluding that "there is no doubt in my mind that the murder was deliberately planned." Justice Maclean then added his observation of Hack during the course of the trial:

> The prisoner's age might be anywhere from twenty-five to thirty-five as far as one can judge from his appearance. He is totally deaf, his deafness resulting as I was given to understand from an attack of measles some six or seven years ago. He can speak, read and write English and German with facility. No suggestion of insanity was put forward at the trial, either of insanity at the time of the offence or insanity at the time of the trial. He appeared to be of average intelligence, reasonably astute, read all the evidence, and conferred with his counsel frequently on matters appearing in the evidence. This of course is from my observation during the trial.

Later in his report, Justice Maclean reiterated that "the accused appeared to be of ordinary intelligence" and then concluded: "I know of no reason from anything that happened at the trial … why the sentence should be commuted." On 14 December, the trial judge received acknowledgment of his report from Lapointe:

> I do not recollect whether I mentioned it to you before, but it is customary for the Minister of Justice to read to his colleagues in Council the Trial Judge's summary in extenso, in order to acquaint them with the salient features of the case … I need not assure you that the summary you have now forwarded, and also your expression of your personal opinion in reference to the commutation of the sentence, will be most useful to me and to my colleagues.

In addition to Justice Maclean's report, the Remission Service had, by this time, the full transcript of the trial. On 20 December, Gallagher sent a telegram to the registrar of the Court of King's Bench requesting copies of all documentary exhibits entered at trial (plans, photographs, receipts, etc.). These were duly sent on the following day.

In their written submissions, both Anderson and the trial judge had referenced Hack's mental condition as a potential reason for granting clemency. Having been alerted that this was likely to be a key factor in the review process, on 28 December, Gallagher wrote to Justice Maclean noting that "examination by alienist is made upon instructions by the Minister of Justice only in exceptional cases especially when important material not available at time of trial is subsequently discovered." The "important material not available at time of trial" consisted of the affidavits testifying to Hack's mental unsoundness that had been submitted by Anderson. With a view to possibly arranging an examination of Hack by an alienist, Gallagher asked Justice Maclean to send a copy of his report to A.L. Geddes, the Saskatchewan deputy attorney general. In a letter to Geddes on the same day, Gallagher noted that the application for commutation in Hack's case was "based principally upon the ground of impaired mentality" and asked Geddes to obtain copies of Anderson's letter and the affidavits. He then continued:

> The Minister of Justice would greatly appreciate your views whether in view of these affidavits the situation calls for an expert mental examination by [an] alienist. And if you think it does he desires to know if you would kindly take the necessary steps to that end [and] appoint an alienist of your choice.

The affidavits were not the only "important material not available at time of trial" bearing on the issue of Hack's mental condition. On 26 December, William Elliott sent Anderson a copy of the petition that had been circulated:

> WHEREAS Mike Hack was found guilty of the murder of George Edey and was sentenced by the Honourable Mr. Justice Maclean to hang on the 9th day of January, 1929, but which said date was extended by order of the Court to the 16th [sic] day of January 1929,
> AND WHEREAS it has been a matter of general knowledge that Mike Hack has been very queer and not of normal mind,
> AND WHEREAS we are of the opinion that at the time of the commission of the said act he was not mentally sound,
> AND WHEREAS we are of the opinion that death penalty [sic] is not the proper punishment for a man in his mental condition, and yet we do not think that it is in the public interest that he should be at large, but rather that the sentence should be commuted to life imprisonment or be committed to a hospital for mentally [sic] defectives,
> WE THEREFORE PETITION THE MINISTER OF JUSTICE OF CANADA that he take these things into consideration and do grant a commutation of the sentence from that of the death penalty to that of imprisonment for life, or that he be committed to a hospital for mentally [sic] defectives.[8]

The petition was signed by seventy-eight local residents, almost all of them from Neudorf. While most of the names are German, several are

British. Two of the signatories (Jacob Niebergall and Philip Armbruster) had also submitted affidavits appealing for clemency. Their affidavits, and those of Dorothea Hack, Fred Hack, and Walter Krahn, could have been sought out and introduced as evidence at the time of the trial. But Elliott clearly could have solicited many more testimonials to Hack's mental condition at that earlier stage of the process, had Anderson elected to make an issue of it at the trial. In his letter to Anderson accompanying the petition, Elliott said that he "could have got several times this number of names if it had been so desired but the names that are on this Petition are practically all the outstanding men in that part of the country and I thought it might be best to confine the Petition to such representative parties." On 29 December, Anderson sent the petition, and Elliott's letter, to Gallagher.

Time was now running out. By 2 January 1929, Geddes had all the materials from both Anderson and Justice Maclean. On 7 January, he messaged Gallagher to inform him that he had engaged Dr. James Walter MacNeill, medical superintendent of the Saskatchewan Hospital at North Battleford, to examine Hack. Dr. MacNeill received his M.D. degree from McGill University in 1901 and practised as a family physician in Saskatchewan from 1906–12. He served as a Liberal member in the Legislative Assembly from 1908–13, after which he travelled to England and the United States to study psychiatry and hospital administration, in preparation for assuming his role as the first superintendent at the North Battleford Mental Hospital, a position he held until 1945.

MacNeill examined Hack at the Regina Jail on 9–11 January and reported his conclusions to Geddes:

> From the history which I obtained both from the Depositions, which you placed at my disposal on the 8th day of January, and which I went through very carefully, and from examination which I made of the Guards who were in charge of the Prisoner in the Jail, I have come to the conclusion that there is something erratic about this man.
>
> I regard him as a Psychopathic personality but I do not regard him as being insane, in the legal acceptation of the word.
>
> There is no doubt in my mind that this man knows the nature and quality of the act for which he was condemned to death, and that he could not be considered as an insane person, but I do regard him as a Psychopathic individual.

Geddes also received the report of Dr. Campbell, who had examined Hack on a number of occasions since July 1928, and did so again at the Regina Jail on 9 January:

The history I have obtained of him from those who have known him is to the effect that he was looked upon as a somewhat peculiar and erratic individual and from my examination of him I would say that he is a psychopathic personality.

In regard to the crime with which he is charged however I would consider him sane, in that he is not, nor has he been, suffering from any delusions as a result of which he would commit this crime. He knows that it is wrong to kill and explains why it is wrong to kill and in so far as I can find out understands the nature and quality of the act with which he is charged.

The reports submitted by the two alienists were strikingly similar in their diagnosis of Hack as a psychopathic personality, their certainty that he was legally sane, and their avoidance of the issue of his "natural imbecility." The alignment of the two reports was, in all likelihood, no coincidence, because they examined their subject on the same day, were well acquainted with one another, and could easily have taken the opportunity to compare notes.

However, there is a further, and darker, possibility. In 1928, Alexander Campbell was an enthusiastic advocate of the eugenics movement, which was at the height of its influence in western Canada through the 1920s and 1930s.[9] During his time at the Weyburn Hospital, Saskatchewan formally adopted two of the measures advocated by the movement for preventing procreation by the feeble-minded.[10] In 1930, the province broadened its mental health laws to authorize the involuntary segregation of "idiots," "imbeciles," or "morons or feeble-minded persons" in provincial institutions. In this, it followed Campbell's proposal that people deemed to be feeble-minded should be "weeded out at childhood and removed to places where contamination of normal people would be impossible."[11] Three years later, the government altered the provincial *Marriage Act* so as to provide that "no one who is an idiot or imbecile" should be allowed to marry. Although Campbell also favoured the third measure – the involuntary sterilization of the feeble-minded – Saskatchewan, unlike its two neighbour provinces to the west, never enacted legislation authorizing this practice.[12]

Campbell had stood ready to testify to Hack's sanity at his trial, though he was never called as a witness because Anderson elected not to make an issue of his client's mental condition. At that stage of the process, Campbell would have known that either a finding of unfitness to stand trial or an acquittal on grounds of insanity would have led to Hack's incarceration in the Weyburn Hospital, certainly for years and quite possibly for life. Then, later, he submitted his testimony of Hack's sanity as part of the clemency application process. At that stage, he would have known that commutation of the death sentence would also have brought Hack to Weyburn. Despite his enthusiasm at that time for the segregation of the feeble-minded, as assistant superintendent of the hospital, Campbell had an incentive to do what he could to prevent that from happening. As noted earlier, by 1928, the Weyburn Hospital, despite having been opened only seven years earlier, was badly overcrowded and understaffed.[13] Much of the population increase in the facility had been driven by admitting more "mental defectives"; between 1923 and 1930, their proportion of total residents rose from 20 per cent to 25 per cent.[14] Furthermore, concerns were beginning to be raised about the considerable drain on the provincial budget caused by the policy of incarcerating such large numbers of the mentally ill and mentally defective.[15] Unlike Alberta, Saskatchewan never made the alternative of sterilization available as a means of relieving overcrowding and keeping costs down. However, in Hack's particular case, there was another alternative. If he were found to be fit to stand trial, and if an insanity defence were to fail at trial, then he was virtually certain to be convicted of murder, with its automatic death sentence. If, upon conviction, his application for commutation of that sentence were to be denied, then he would be hanged. That meant that there was a potential means of "weeding him out" of the general population that would be cheap and final, and would not require finding space for him at Weyburn.

Campbell therefore had two reasons – one eugenic and one administrative – for preferring Hack's conviction to his acquittal and for preferring his execution to commutation of his sentence. Moreover, he had two opportunities to pursue these objectives, the first at trial and the second during the clemency process, by testifying to Hack's sanity and suppressing any mention of his "natural imbecility." It would also have been easy for him to recruit a colleague in charge of another overcrowded and understaffed mental institution to help push the case in the same direction. The joint weight of their opinions could have been countered only by assessments of Hack by independent, out-of-province alienists. But Anderson never sought such assessments.

The foregoing hypothesis is, of course, highly speculative; like Hack's conviction, it is based entirely on circumstantial evidence. There is no way to establish, with any certainty, Campbell's motivation for neglecting to determine the extent of Hack's mental deficiency, nor for attesting with such conviction that he was legally sane. But it is possible that it was not an entirely disinterested expert opinion.

In any event, Geddes sent the reports he had received from Campbell and MacNeill to Gallagher on 14 January. He had previously also forwarded a letter of 4 January from Herbert Sampson, the Crown prosecutor in the trial, who said of Hack that "while it may be that he is not particularly bright, as one can scarcely say that a bright person would think that he could commit such an offence ... and get away with it, yet the murder [was] deliberately planned, and for the purpose of getting possession of Edey's horses." Along with Sampson's letter, Geddes also sent the report received from Dr. Rothwell of the Regina Jail that "Hack appears to be in a normal state of mind and there does not appear to be any of the usual symptoms of insanity."

By 14 January, therefore, Gallagher was in possession of assessments by MacNeill, Campbell, and Rothwell, plus the observations made during the trial by the judge and Crown prosecutor – all agreeing that, while not particularly bright, Hack was not legally insane. In support of the application for clemency, Gallagher had the opinions of Anderson and Elliott, plus the testimony of seventy-eight local residents who were familiar with Hack, to the effect that he was mentally unsound. It was an unequal contest. The conclusion of Gallagher's memorandum for the minister of justice, prepared on 14 January, was therefore unsurprising:

> After a careful analysis of all of the evidence adduced at the trial, and considering all relevant material now on record, the undersigned is of opinion that the law may well be allowed to take its course.

At this point, the minister had two options available, either of which would have saved Hack from his 18 January date with the hangman. On the one hand, he could have rejected Gallagher's advice and recommended commutation of the sentence to the governor general. Alternatively, Lapointe had the authority to order a new trial, or to refer the case to the provincial court of appeal, on the ground that "important material not available at time of trial [has been] subsequently discovered." In that case, the question of Hack's sanity would be put to a jury to decide.

Lapointe did neither. Instead, he sent Justice Maclean's report, the trial transcript, and "other documents relating to the case" to the governor general, concluding: "Upon careful examination of all which, the undersigned respectfully recommends that the law be allowed to take its course." It is not clear whether the "other documents" mentioned included the testimonials of Hack's mental unsoundness.

The Order-in-Council was issued on 15 January:

> The circumstances of the case having been fully considered by the Governor General in Council, together with the Report of the Minister of Justice adverse to the commutation of said sentence.
>
> The Governor General is unable to order any interference with the sentence of the Court.

The denial of clemency was immediately communicated to Martin Wilkinson, sheriff of the judicial district of Regina, as well as to Anderson, Elliott, and Justice Maclean. It was further conveyed to the condemned man on the same day by Rev. C.T. Wetzstein, a Lutheran minister who was his spiritual advisor.

The failure of Hack's clemency application was not inevitable. As mentioned earlier, during the period when the death penalty was mandatory, about 40 per cent of such requests were successful. In 1928, the year of Hack's trial, the odds were even better: of 19 death sentences handed down that year, only six were carried out (including Hack's), while seven were commuted. Some of the responsibility for the failure of the application must be laid at the feet of the trial judge. The opinion of Hack's mental condition expressed by Justice Maclean in his report to the Remission Service – that he was "of average intelligence," "reasonably astute," and "of ordinary intelligence" – was based entirely, as he himself said, on his observation of the accused during the trial. As noted earlier, contemporary reports tell us that during the process of jury selection, "Hack sat in the prisoner's box ... keeping his eyes for the most part on the judge. As Anderson challenged prospective jurors, Hack leaned over the rail of the box and scrutinized the list that his counsel held in his hand. He looked in turn at the jurors as they came up to be sworn." Then, later in the proceedings, "Hack sat motionless as the evidence unfolded, apparently oblivious to all around him. Leaning on the right rail of the prisoner's box, he gave verbal answers to his lawyers as they wrote out questions for him at intervals." The accused, therefore, may have given every appearance of being "of average intelligence" and "reasonably astute," and may have seemed to be "read[ing] all the evidence, and conferr[ing] with his counsel frequently on matters appearing in the evidence," while actually having, as Anderson said of his client, "a low order of mentality which did not duly appreciate what was transpiring."

In light of the importance attached in the review process to the trial judge's report and recommendation concerning clemency, if Justice Maclean had offered the contrary opinion that there were doubts about Hack's mental soundness, it is very likely that the sentence would have been commuted. To stop there, however, would be to pin the blame for the adverse outcome solely on the trial judge and to ignore the roles played by others. One of the principal others was Anderson.

The trial judge based his opinion of Hack's intelligence and astuteness solely on his observation of Hack's behaviour throughout the trial, because he had no other evidence to take into account. He had no other evidence because Anderson called no witnesses who might provide such evidence. Because Anderson did not seek an application to have Hack declared unfit to stand trial or attempt an insanity defence, he had no reason to call witnesses who could testify that Hack was "very queer and not of normal mind." More to the point, he had no reason to call as expert witnesses one or more alienists who could attest to Hack's degree of feeble-mindedness, whether on the basis of IQ testing or some alternative investigative procedure. As we saw in the previous chapter, either an application for a declaration of unfitness or an insanity defence might not have succeeded (though the former was more likely to succeed than the latter). But had either been attempted, then evidence that Hack was mentally unsound would have been on the record, and the trial judge would have been compelled to mention it in his report. More importantly, he would have had a much better evidentiary basis for drawing his own conclusion about Hack's state of mind, and would not have been able to declare him of average or ordinary intelligence just because he seemed to be following the course of the trial attentively. The best case would have been for either judge or jury to recommend clemency in Hack's case, and either party might have done so had they heard the evidence from the defence. But even failing that, had there been any indication in the trial judge's report that Hack might not be mentally sound, then that fact would, in all likelihood, have found its way into the memo prepared for the minister by Gallagher, the chief clerk of the Remission Service. These doubts might well have sufficed for the minister of justice to recommend to Cabinet that Hack's death sentence be commuted, and for Cabinet to act on that recommendation.

Though his own assessment of Hack's mental condition was prejudicial to the clemency application, Justice Maclean did alert the minister that there was an issue here that they might want to pursue. In his letter of 15 November to the under secretary of state, the trial judge said: "No suggestion of insanity, either at the time of the trial or at the time of the commission of the offence, was made by counsel for the accused. Counsel, however, did state that the department would be asked to enquire into the mentality of the prisoner. *I presume that this would be done in any event, whether requested or not*" (emphasis added). Justice Maclean repeated this point in his report: "After the verdict, before sentence, counsel for the prisoner intimated that he would make some representations to the Department of Justice, asking that an enquiry be made into the mentality of the prisoner. *I presume that will be done whether asked for or not; and any report so made after such enquiry will be more conclusive than any opinion I have on that point*" (emphasis added).

In both these documents, Maclean stated that Hack *appeared to be* of average or ordinary intelligence, based on his observation of him during the trial, seemingly suggesting that a more authoritative assessment would be in order. For what it is worth, the Crown prosecutor was not being helpful at this point. In his letter of 4 January 1929 to the Saskatchewan deputy attorney general, Sampson wrote: "In view of the opinions of Dr. Campbell and Rothwell, as already intimated, and nothing having occurred at the trial which would change such opinions, I really cannot see any particular necessity for any further examination by an alienist."

As far as can be determined, Anderson made no request for an examination of Hack by an alienist during the clemency process. However, as Justice Maclean intimates, a request should not have been necessary. Gallagher's memorandum to Lapointe of 22 November includes the following information on the procedures followed by the Remission Service:

> The Judge, of course, forwards his report to Ottawa as soon as at all possible, in order that the Minister of Justice may have time to investigate, - *direct examinations by experts to determine mental impairment when advisable*, - analyze evidence, - call meeting of Council to consider it, - submit to His Excellency the Governor General, etc., etc., etc. (emphasis added)

The minister, therefore, was empowered to have Hack examined by an alienist in the absence of a request by defence counsel and in the absence of any evidence of his mental unsoundness being adduced at trial. In its 1956 report, the Joint Committee claimed that this step was routine: "Where there is the slightest question of mental abnormality, special psychiatric reports are obtained from consulting psychiatrists employed by the Remission Service. In addition, careful consideration is given to the representations of defence counsel and friends and all points of fact and detail raised are carefully investigated to ensure that no factor favouring clemency is overlooked."[16] The Committee also reported that "mental abnormality falling short of the legal defence of insanity is a frequent factor in commutation ..."[17] Needless to say, there was a question of mental abnormality in Hack's case, based on representations from defence counsel and seventy-eight local residents.

It was on this basis that Gallagher, acting on behalf of the minister of justice, asked Geddes, the Saskatchewan deputy attorney general, to arrange examination of Hack by an alienist. Unfortunately for the appellants, that examination, conducted by Dr. James MacNeill, concluded that Hack was not insane "in the legal acceptation of the word." The expert opinions of Drs. Campbell, Rothwell, and MacNeill stood unopposed, due to the fact that at no point – neither in pursuit of a declaration of unfitness to stand trial, nor in the service of a defence of insanity at trial, nor to support the application for clemency after the conclusion of the trial – did Anderson seek out an expert opinion of the nature and severity of Hack's intellectual disability. Aside from his brief mention that Hack was "under observation by Dr. Campbell of the Weyburn Mental Hospital" (who we know would not have been helpful at any stage), there is no indication that Anderson ever considered having Hack examined by a qualified alienist. Even after deciding not to pursue an unfitness application or an insanity defence, he could – and should – have sought such an assessment to support his application for clemency. Had he done so, and had he received a diagnosis of even moderate mental subnormality, then that evidence would also have had to be taken seriously by Gallagher and by Lapointe and could well have led to a different outcome.

Once again, now at this post-conviction stage of the judicial process, Hack received ineffective assistance from Anderson. Hack's conviction was a miscarriage of justice by virtue of the fact that there was evidence of his cognitive disability – some ready at hand, more that could have been recruited – which, had it been introduced at trial, would have had a reasonable probability of leading either to a declaration of unfitness to stand trial or to an acquittal by reason of insanity. During the clemency process, the same evidence, had it been adduced, would have had at least a reasonable probability of leading to commutation of his death sentence. Not just one miscarriage of justice, then, but two.

One might wonder whether it is appropriate to speak of a miscarriage of *justice* in the clemency context, since the granting of clemency was a matter of mercy (the exercise of a prerogative) rather than of justice.[18] To put it otherwise, commutation of their death sentence was not an outcome of the clemency process to which the convicted murderer had a *right*. Notwithstanding this perfectly valid point, the use of the same language serves to highlight the crucial commonality between the trial and post-trial processes in the case of Hack: the ineffective assistance rendered by Anderson. There was a reasonable probability, in each process, that Anderson's failure to adduce persuasive evidence of Hack's cognitive disability had a material impact on the outcome, to his client's detriment: in the trial process, conviction; in the clemency process, execution. Hack may not have had a right to commutation of his sentence, but he did have a right that his counsel do his job, both at trial and afterward.

Anderson's failure to recruit expert opinions of Hack's mental condition to support the application for clemency is especially tragic, because the three reports that were submitted to Gallagher and Lapointe were all deeply flawed. To see why, we need to recall the *Criminal Code* tests of legal insanity in place at the time:

> 19(1) No person shall be convicted of an offence by reason of an act done or omitted by him when labouring under natural imbecility, or disease of the mind, to such an extent as to render him incapable of appreciating the nature and quality of the act or omission, and of knowing that such act or omission was wrong.

One problem with the reports by Drs. Campbell, Rothwell, and MacNeill is that they all pronounced on the issue of Hack's sanity. But sanity (or insanity) is a legal concept, not a medical one. The sanity of the accused is therefore a question to be decided by a judge or a jury, not a medical expert. The three physicians were entitled to express opinions as to Hack's mental deficiency or mental illness, but not on the further question of his capacity to appreciate the nature and quality of his act or to know that it was wrong. Expert witnesses may give evidence only within the field in which they are qualified, and the qualifications of these three witnesses were medical, not legal.[19] In addressing the legal issue, they were out of their lane.

But even on matters within the scope of their expertise, they addressed the wrong question. The law establishes two distinct grounds for an insanity defence: "natural imbecility, or disease of the mind." The reference to "disease of the mind" invokes the familiar category of mental illness, especially some kind of psychosis that deprives the offender of the capacity either to appreciate what they are doing or to know that it is wrong. (I continue to assume that "or" is the correct conjunction here, rather than "and.") Quite clearly, psychosis was the kind of condition that the three medical experts were looking for when they examined Hack.

It is doubtful that Rothwell actually qualified as an expert concerning mental illnesses, because he was a general physician with no specialized training as an alienist. Furthermore, his "examination" of Hack consisted of his observations of him during the period of Hack's confinement in the Regina Jail. But in any case, when Rothwell reported the absence of "any of the usual symptoms of insanity," we may assume that what he had in mind were signs of psychosis: disordered thinking, delusions, lack of grip on reality, etc. As far as can be determined, at no time in his life did Hack exhibit any of these symptoms (except for the ones he appears to have feigned when examined by Campbell on 30 September). His mental impairment was of a different sort: not a "disease of the mind" but "natural imbecility." There is no evidence that Rothwell ever examined Hack with that kind of diagnosis in mind, or administered any tests that would have determined whether his intelligence was markedly subnormal.

By contrast, Campbell was a trained alienist and did examine Hack on numerous occasions, both before and after his trial. In his report submitted to Gallagher, Campbell stated that "he is not, nor has he been, suffering from any delusions as a result of which he would commit this crime." Campbell was evidently also looking for signs of psychosis. MacNeill reached the same conclusion, based on his examination of Hack on 9 January 1929: the prisoner "could not be considered as an insane person." There is no evidence that either alienist examined Hack with a view to determining whether he suffered from "natural imbecility," for instance, by administering an IQ test.

With the exception of Campbell's observation that he was "not of a particularly bright type," neither of these experts addressed the condition that was attested to by those who were most familiar with Hack: that he had the mentality, and the volatile temper, of a child. As Anderson was convinced on this question, referring to Hack's "low order of mentality," what he needed was the testimony of experts who would submit Hack to IQ tests to determine just how subnormal his intelligence was. If a case could be made that he did indeed suffer from "natural imbecility," then this expert evidence would have stood unopposed by the medical reports by Drs. Rothwell, Campbell, and MacNeill, none of whom spoke to this question.

Though Drs. Campbell and MacNeill did not address the question of "natural imbecility," and though both attested that Hack was quite sane, they also both diagnosed him as a psychopath. This is rather odd, to say the least, because they must not have regarded psychopathy as a "disease of the mind" for the purpose of determining legal insanity, despite the fact that, etymologically, "psychopathy" means "disease of the mind." Neither of them was very forthcoming about their understanding of the nature of psychopathy (both seemed to base their diagnosis on the fact that Hack was "erratic"). They may have had nothing specific in mind by the term, using it to cover any of a wide range of personality disorders. The first *Diagnostic and Statistical Manual of Mental Disorders* was not published until 1952. Psychopathy was included as a mental disorder up to the third edition (1980) but was subsequently omitted in the fourth (1994) and fifth (2013) editions. Nowadays psychopathy is usually thought of as a personality disorder marked by symptoms such as deficient emotional responses, lack of empathy, and disinhibition, commonly resulting in persistent antisocial and/or criminal behaviour. If Campbell and MacNeill had this specific diagnosis in mind, then they might have been expected to doubt whether Hack had the capacity to understand the wrongness of his act, as psychopaths were commonly thought to lack effective guidance by conscience. MacNeill did not address this question in his report, but Campbell did, stating that Hack "knows that it is wrong to kill and explains why it is wrong to kill." If both alienists truly regarded Hack as a psychopath, then they might have wondered just how thoroughly he was capable of internalizing and operationalizing this moral "knowledge."

# 8
# January 1929

During the time that the death penalty was in place in Canada, hanging was the only permitted means of carrying it out.[1] Although other means were considered from time to time, they were never adopted. In 1956, the joint parliamentary committee tasked with reviewing the death penalty recommended its retention, but also recommended that hanging be replaced by electrocution or the use of a gas chamber.[2] This recommendation was never acted on by the government of the day. Instead, the lengthy career of the death penalty came to an inevitable end. In 1961, possibly in response to the Truscott case, the government introduced the category of non-capital murder, and in 1963, Cabinet began to routinely commute death sentences. Thirteen years later, capital punishment was abolished, except for certain military offences under the *National Defence Act*.

Mike Hack's execution was originally scheduled for 9 January 1929, but it had to be postponed for nine days because the hangman, Arthur Ellis, was otherwise engaged. "Arthur Ellis" was actually the pseudonym of Arthur Bartholomew English, who began his career in England and adopted the surname of his uncle, John Ellis, also a well-established hangman. In the early years of the twentieth century, Ellis established a reputation as an experienced and efficient executioner in the Middle East, and in 1913, he was invited to become Canada's official hangman. Over the course of his lengthy career, he claimed to have carried out more than 600 hangings. He used the English "long drop" method, developed by William Marwood, which required a careful calculation of the condemned person's body weight and the length of rope necessary to achieve instantaneous death by dislocating the neck, rather than a slower death by strangulation.[3] However, he eschewed use of the Marwood noose, whose efficiency for this purpose had been proven in England. Instead, he stuck with the traditional hangman's knot behind the victim's left ear, which resulted in as many strangulation deaths as dislocations.

Ellis's working outfit was a frock coat with striped trousers, often with a flower pinned to his lapel. He did not conceal his identity, indeed was rather proud of his line of work. His last hanging occurred in 1935, when he bungled the execution of Tomasina Sarao in Montreal. His practice had been to visit the condemned person in jail the day before the execution to determine body weight. However, Ms. Sarao was not in the Bordeaux Jail that afternoon; she was being held instead at the women's jail on Fullam Street. Not able to weigh her himself, Ellis was given a slip of paper on which her weight had been recorded. Unbeknownst to him, however, this figure represented her weight when she was first committed to prison, and she had put on an additional forty pounds since. As a result of this miscalculation, she dropped too far once the trap door was sprung and was decapitated.[4] This catastrophe put an end to the practice of allowing the public to get tickets to watch hangings. It also put an end to Ellis's career. He was never actually fired; instead, he was quietly boycotted: sheriffs simply stopped sending him work. Ellis died in poverty in Montreal three years later, apparently of an alcohol-related disease, and was buried in Mount Royal Cemetery.

During January, Hack was passing his final days in the Regina Jail, under the jurisdiction of Sheriff Martin Wilkinson and Warden Tom Hayes. The jail was constructed in 1913 on a site three miles northeast of Regina, with accommodation for 150 prisoners with sentences of less than two years; those with longer sentences were sent to the Saskatchewan Penitentiary in Prince Albert. Ellis had campaigned for every province to designate one central site for executions, possibly to simplify his travels across the country. Saskatchewan had complied with this request, and the Regina Jail had been selected as that site. Parts of the original structure continued in use until 2006, when they were demolished to make way for the Regina Correctional Centre, which stands today on the same site.

The Order-in-Council denying the application for clemency was received by Wilkinson and passed on to Hayes shortly after noon on January 15. Hayes in turn passed the news on to Rev. C.T. Wetzstein, a Lutheran minister who was Hack's spiritual advisor. When Hack asked Wetzstein, "Is there any news of my case?," Wetzstein took a pencil and a pad of paper and wrote "You have lost. The Government will not interfere in the sentence." Hack read the note, crumpled the paper in his hand, and walked back into his cell. He showed little emotion at the news.[5]

8.1. Regina Jail

Source: Saskatchewan Archives

8.2. Regina Jail scaffold

Source: Saskatchewan Archives

All day long on 16 January, workmen were hammering on the scaffold that was being constructed in the jail's narrow inside courtyard. The noises ceased in the afternoon when Ellis came to examine the structure, test the drop, and work out how much rope he would need to give the condemned man. Once it was clear that the execution would be going ahead, Hack was watched night and day by three warders. His belt was taken away from him and the laces removed from his shoes, lest he be tempted to try suicide.

Suicide, however, seemed to be the last thing on his mind. He approached his impending death with remarkable equanimity, spending his time reading his Bible, underlining passages that had particular significance for him, and writing a series of farewell letters, including these five:

To the Rev. J. Fritz, pastor of Trinity Evangelical Lutheran Church (in German):

*I thank you most heartily for your kindness to send me so many nice books. I inform you that I go in peace to the other world because it is the will of God that I should be with him and his holy angels ... I was born 16 March 1901, in Lemberg, Sask., and I die on the 18th of January, 1929, in Regina Jail. Innocently [underscored] I must give my life for another murderer ... I pity my dear mother on her sickbed, being 66 years old, living near Neudorf, also two brothers, five sisters, and over 82 other relatives ... I have reached an age of 27 years, 10 months, and 2 days. I was sick for seven years and deaf for the last six years. I have led many to God, was well read in the Bible, and believed with a firm faith in the divine God ...*[6]

To his sister Dora and brother-in-law George Hepting (in German):

*I want to write you my last letter and wish you God's blessing, so long I live. While I'm going to another world and I'd like to share with you and tell you and wish you God's blessing, and may God take care of you, whatever may happen ... I wish that you stay close to God so long you live and take care of the mother, so long she lives, in her old age and that she has her daily bread. I can't help my mother no longer, and if it's God's will that he wants to take me from here, I'm ready to go. There's nothing on this world anyway but anger, hostility, sickness, and injustice. But by God we live our peace, and a better life than I had here. 7 years I was sick, 6 years deaf, and 3 times close to death. But now comes my last death, but I'm not afraid, I trust in God, He wants it that way. I close my letter with greetings from my whole heart and all of you. Don't be sad about me because we won't see us in this world but in heavenly paradise. God the Lord be with you all time. Good bye, good bye till we meet again.*[7]

To William McGill, a fellow prisoner whose death sentence was up for review (in English):

> I have taken care of everything for everybody, my guards, my dear watchman and for you. Don't worry anymore about me in the arms of Jesus I will be for ever and ever ... Now comes Mr. Ellis to take me out. I can tell you now just as much as I've been able to tell you before, I am prepared to go. I feel very good and I'm about ready to go up to Jesus. He is coming to meet me. Up in the sky my soul will fly.

To Warden Hayes (in English):

> I write only a few lines for my last time to say I thank you for the trouble I have put you to in jail and for the kind way you have treated me. If I have done something wrong I wish you to please forgive me for everything. You was my best friend ever since I entered the jail, so kind to me while I was here. The house warden and guards here were very kind to me also and I cannot say anything bad. I will soon go to the new world. God be with you for ever and ever. I go to the new place Friday morning and I forgive everybody.
>
> Postscript: I was born on a farm three miles east of Lemberg, sec. 14, range 9, township 20, on March 16, 1901. Age 27 years, 10 months and 2 days.

Finally, to the public (in English):

> Friday is my last day. By the grace of God I hope to meet my death quietly and resign to the will of my kind, heavenly father ... It is true I am a sinner and as such justly under condemnation, but here is my Lord, Jesus Christ, who has redeemed me from the guilt of sin and has earned righteousness for me in which I stand before God. I am prepared to leave all behind and accept in exchange the eternal life which Christ has promised me for ever and ever ...
>
> Mike Haack
>
> Born on March 16, 1901
> Died on January 18, 1929
> Age 27–10–2
> Thanks everybody for everything they have done for me.[8]

The morning of Friday 18 January was clear and cold. Hack had spent the night with Rev. Wetzstein reading his Bible and reciting prayers and hymns. During the 1920s, it became standard practice to hold executions during the early morning hours, so as not to disturb the daily routines of the other prisoners in the jail. At about 2:00 a.m., Mike Hack ate his last meal: meat, potatoes, vegetables, coffee, and bread. He was

8.3. Percy Anderson's headstone
Source: Photo by author

called by the warden shortly before the appointed hour of 4:45 a.m. He was dressed in rough khaki trousers, a collarless khaki shirt, coarse gray socks, and unlaced black shoes. His final words were to thank his jailers and bid them goodbye. His arms were pinioned, and he was led to the gallows by the hangman. They mounted thirteen snow-coated steps in the dark, and Hack was positioned on the trap. His ankles were bound, and the black hood and noose were adjusted. He did not say a word. The words of the Apostles' Creed were recited by Rev. Wetzstein and then the phrase "Create in him a clean heart, O God." At that moment, precisely at 4:43 a.m., the trap dropped.

On this occasion, evidently, Ellis did his job properly. Dr. Rothwell examined the body and pronounced death. A coroner's jury of six "good and lawful men" certified that the sentence of death had been duly carried out. On the same day, Sheriff Wilkinson notified the secretary of state in Ottawa of the execution. Hack's body was then taken to Speers Funeral Home, where brief funeral services were held for the

8.4. Site of Mike Hack's grave
Source: Photo by author

family at 11:00 a.m., with Rev. Wetzstein officiating. Mike Hack was then buried in an unmarked grave in Regina Cemetery.

The cemetery occupies a large rectangle of land north of the Regina city centre, and just east of the CanAm Highway. Its road system, laid out as a grid, divides the terrain into ranges of numbered blocks. Individual graves are identified by their block and plot numbers. In the east-central area of the cemetery – plot 26, in block 345 – can be found a handsome brown granite headstone with the inscription "Percy McCuaig Anderson, 1879–1948." About a hundred meters to the north – plot 13 of block 292 – the spot where Hack was buried remains a featureless open stretch of grass. No marker was ever erected on his grave.

# 9
# The Bigger Picture

The criminal justice process in the case of Mike Hack occupied 256 days from his arrest on 8 May 1928 to his execution on 18 January 1929. Hack himself was responsible for initiating that process, through his brutal, unprovoked, and pointless murder of George Edey. But once the process was underway, its subsequent course was driven by other players, each of whom made key decisions at key junctures – decisions that, had they been different, could have made the difference between acquittal and conviction, or between commutation and execution. Therefore, in retrospect, it is tempting to imagine the alternative universe in which things might have gone otherwise.

If only ...

    ... the jury, which correctly convicted Mike Hack based on the evidence presented at trial, had recommended mercy in his case.

    ... Justice Maclean had recommended mercy, or at least had not insisted so strenuously in his trial report that Mike Hack was mentally normal.

    ... Herbert Sampson had not similarly insisted on Mike Hack's mental normality in his input into the clemency process.

    ... Alexander Campbell had tested the accused for "natural imbecility" before his trial.

    ... either Alexander Campbell or James MacNeill had tested Mike Hack for "natural imbecility" as part of the clemency process.

    ... either Alexander Campbell or James MacNeill had not insisted that Mike Hack was legally sane.

    ... Michael Gallagher had assigned greater weight to the evidence before him of Mike Hack's intellectual disability.

    ... Ernest Lapointe had declined to follow Michael Gallagher's recommendation that the law be allowed to take its course.

... William Elliott had prevailed on Percy Anderson to mount a more effective defence and found local witnesses willing to testify at trial to Mike Hack's mental deficiency.

... Percy Anderson had elected to make an issue of Mike Hack's mental condition at trial, either by applying for a declaration of unfitness to stand trial or by mounting an insanity defence, and had marshalled the necessary testimony, both lay and expert, of his "natural imbecility."

... Percy Anderson had solicited expert opinion of Mike Hack's "natural imbecility" in support of the application for clemency.

Had any of these parties acted otherwise than they did, the eventual outcome might itself have been otherwise. Of all the actors in the drama, however, Percy Anderson bears the heaviest individual responsibility for that outcome. If we seek a simple explanation of how Mike Hack came to be hanged, then it is entirely fair to highlight the role played by Anderson, who rendered ineffective assistance at both the trial and post-trial stages.

However, to confine ourselves solely to the contributions of the various individual actors would be to miss an important dimension of the story. Eve Brensike Primus has usefully proposed distinguishing instances of ineffective assistance along two axes: personal v. structural, and episodic v. pervasive.[1] These axes intersect, yielding four categories of cases. Counsel's ineffectiveness is personal if the deficiency is entirely their own: they fail to look up an important point of law or to carry out a factual investigation. The ineffectiveness is structural if it results from circumstances beyond counsel's control: the trial judge prevents them from mounting an effective defence or their client refuses to consult with them. The other axis looks to the breadth of counsel's deficient performance at trial. It is episodic if the failures are limited to isolated occurrences within a generally good performance: a missed point of order or failure to file a motion. The deficient performance is pervasive if it compromises the whole of the defence: counsel frequently falls asleep during the proceedings or is abusing drugs or alcohol.

In terms of these categories, Percy Anderson's ineffectiveness was clearly pervasive: his failure at trial to seek a declaration of unfitness or attempt an insanity defence – or, indeed, to call any witnesses at all – cost his client any chance of acquittal; his failure to seek out expert testimony to Mike Hack's intellectual impairment cost him any chance of clemency. The more interesting question is the extent to which it was personal or structural. Brensike Primus herself observes that "structural ineffectiveness can ... be the product of the indigent defense delivery system," citing the instance of an attorney who "must handle 19,000 cases in a year (which would give her only seven minutes for the average case)."[2]

The evidence of Mike Hack's finances heard at trial showed conclusively that he was an indigent client, without the resources to pay for a lawyer of Percy Anderson's status and reputation. His family, if so disposed, might have been able to engage the services of William Elliott, the local barrister from Neudorf who had acted for them in the matter of Mathias's estate, but they too would have been unable to manage Percy Anderson's fees. Hence, he must have been engaged under the terms of an "indigent defence delivery system."

Such systems are in place today. Under the constitutional division of powers, the federal government has jurisdiction over criminal law, while the administration of justice falls to the provinces. In the interest of ensuring access to justice, the federal government can (and does) contribute to the cost of legal aid programs, but the design and administration of those programs is a provincial responsibility. Consequently, Canada has thirteen different indigent defence delivery systems (ten for the provinces and three for the territories). However, they all operate on either of two main models, or a mix of both: private bar, in which lawyers in private practice are issued certificates to provide services to clients, or staff lawyer, in which the services are provided by salaried lawyers employed directly by the legal aid plan, often distributed throughout the province in community law offices.[3]

These centralized systems for the delivery of legal aid are a relatively recent historical development. The first formal plan in Canada was introduced in Ontario in 1967,[4] and Saskatchewan initiated its staff lawyer plan in 1974.[5] From 1967 to 1974, the province relied on a private bar system administered by the Saskatchewan Law Society, the terms of which allowed the government to pay relatively modest fees to lawyers who volunteered to provide criminal defence. Prior to 1967, the province's private bar system had no central administrative body. Instead, when indigent defendants faced serious criminal charges, such as murder, the trial judge could assign competent counsel from private practice to provide defence.[6] Prior to 1949, lawyers were remunerated for their services only in murder cases.[7] In that year, this arrangement was extended to defendants facing other criminal charges, but at a lower rate of remuneration. As of 1949, the rate of compensation was $50 to $75 per trial day; in 1928 it would presumably have been much lower than that. According to one commentator, the payment was "rarely commensurate with the amount of work involved."[8] No disbursement was offered to counsel to cover travel, subsistence, accommodation, or any of the collateral expenses of preparing the defence, such as engaging or interviewing witnesses.[9]

Percy Anderson would have been assigned to defend Mike Hack on this basis.[10] Anderson was a busy man: between April and November 1928, he argued seven cases before the Saskatchewan Court of Appeal. Having these more glamorous, and doubtless more remunerative, assignments on board, defending Hack was probably a low priority for him, despite it being a capital case. It was not helpful that the case was being tried out in the boondocks, some ninety miles from Regina. One commentator observes that the Saskatchewan indigent defence system "worked most unsatisfactorily in rural areas due to the paucity of available lawyers with criminal expertise combined with an inadequate fee schedule that did not compensate for travelling time."[11] Either applying to have Hack declared unfit to stand trial or raising an insanity defence would have significantly extended the process and engaged much more of Anderson's valuable time, without adequate compensation. Either strategy would also have required soliciting expert witnesses and interviewing local witnesses (though presumably William Elliott could have taken on some of these latter tasks), without any compensation whatever.

Just to be clear, the indigent defence system in place at the time did not always let accused murderers down. The defendants fared better in two other Saskatchewan murder trials of the late 1920s. In May 1928, Ernest Olson was charged with the murder of William Robson, a farmer for whom he had once worked.[12] Olson was an indigent client who could not afford to engage defence counsel. His trial was scheduled for 30 October in the Court of King's Bench in the town of Melfort, about 170 miles due north of Regina. On the morning of that day, Bert Keown, a Melfort-based criminal lawyer, was called to the courthouse to represent Olson at trial. Keown had never met the man and had no knowledge of the case. Based on his quickly arranged interview of Olson, he concluded that his client was mentally subnormal and unable to instruct counsel. A jury was then struck to determine whether Olson was fit to stand trial. Dr. James MacNeill, he of the North Battleford Mental Hospital, submitted an expert opinion that Olson was feebleminded, with a mental age of about eight or nine, and that he would be unable to understand the trial proceedings. Notwithstanding this evidence, the jury found him fit for trial.

As with Mike Hack, the evidence presented at trial implicating Olson in Robson's murder was entirely circumstantial. The most damaging testimony was given by Robson's estranged wife, who, until about six weeks prior to the murder, had been cohabiting with Olson. She claimed that Olson had told her that he had killed Robson and his housekeeper with an axe and then burned down the farmhouse, with both bodies inside. It took the jury only two hours on the second day of the trial to render a verdict of guilty.

Keown intended to appeal the verdict, challenging the jury's finding of fitness to stand trial. However, rather than conduct the appeal himself, he turned for assistance to a criminal lawyer based in Prince Albert, about 60 miles to the northwest, who had been practising law for only nine years but who had already managed to make quite a name for himself in the courtroom. That lawyer was John George Diefenbaker, later to achieve wider fame as the thirteenth prime minister of Canada. Diefenbaker pointed out to Keown that they could not dispute the jury's verdict of fitness because, however ill-grounded it might be, it involved no mistake of law. However, at the appeal, he did vigorously pursue issues concerning the trial judge's handling of the process, especially his intervention during Keown's cross-examination of Mrs. Olson, in which he loudly proclaimed that she was telling the truth. Despite Diefenbaker's best efforts, the appeal court found no miscarriage of justice.

The story, however, did not end there. Though it did not constitute grounds for appeal, the justices did question the jury's verdict of fitness, especially its disregard of MacNeill's expert testimony, and they recommended that the medical evidence be included in the subsequent application for clemency. Diefenbaker did just that, and in January 1929, Olson's death sentence was commuted to life in the Prince Albert penitentiary.

Diefenbaker had similar success a year later with another indigent client, in a case that had even more similarities with that of Mike Hack. In August 1929, John Pasowesty was charged with the murder of his father, who owned a cattle farm near the town of Wynyard, some 150 miles southeast of Prince Albert.[13] This time, Diefenbaker conducted the defence from the beginning. The trial began at the Court of King's Bench at Wynyard on 19 November. Herbert Sampson appeared for the Crown. Diefenbaker had to contend with a trial judge, Justice George E. Taylor, who was renowned for his partiality towards the prosecution. Once again, the evidence against the accused was circumstantial, but despite his best efforts, Diefenbaker was unable to secure an acquittal. As with Olson, his subsequent appeal of the verdict was unsuccessful.

However, Diefebaker had been aware from the beginning that his client was mentally deficient. Despite having learned at the time of the preliminary inquiry that the Crown had evidence that Pasowesty had the intelligence of a ten-year-old boy, Diefenbaker for some reason had elected not to seek a finding of unfitness to stand trial or attempt a defence of mental disorder at trial. As with Mike Hack, the Crown had anticipated such a defence and had lined up medical experts prepared to testify to Pasowesty's sanity. In another parallel with the Hack case, the trial judge had gone on record as stating that, although the defendant was only seventeen years of age, "his development, mentally as well as physically, appears to be considerably beyond that age."[14]

John Pasowesty was sentenced to hang on 21 February 1930. The chances of a successful application for clemency appeared slim. However, Diefenbaker was able to arrange for prominent alienists to examine his client – alienists who, based on their examination, confirmed his feeble-mindedness. On 17 February, the federal Cabinet granted a three-week extension of the execution date to allow for further examination of Pasowesty's mental condition. On 4 March, Pasowesty's sentence was commuted, largely based on the evidence that Diefenbaker had solicited and submitted.

The contrast between the performances of Percy Anderson and John Diefenbaker on behalf of their indigent clients is stark. Both had to travel considerable distances from their home base to conduct the defence, and both were working within the financial constraints of the indigent defence system. While neither was able to secure an acquittal at trial, or on appeal, only Diefenbaker invested the time and labour necessary for a successful clemency application, especially in the case of Pasowesty. Applying Brensike Primus's categories, we could therefore say that Percy Anderson's various failures – to seek a finding of unfitness for Mike Hack, or to raise an insanity defence on his behalf at trial, or to marshal the expert evidence necessary to support his clemency application – were all personal, because, as the example of Diefenbaker shows, it was within his power to do much better. But these failures can equally be seen as structural, resulting from official arrangements for indigent defence that systematically disadvantaged defendants who were both poor and rural. Under the system in place at the time, Ernest Olson and John Pasowesty got lucky: they drew defence counsel willing to do whatever was necessary to save them from hanging. Mike Hack did not.

There has been no systematic study of the influence of defendants' social class or income level on the disposition of capital murder cases in Canada. Studies of murder cases in an American jurisdiction have yielded the result that the socioeconomic status of the accused appears not to matter in its own right, unless the victim of the crime is of higher status (which George Edey was not).[15] However, it can play a role in a more indirect way, in so far as it bears on the defendant's ability to hire defence counsel – a US study has concluded that hired counsel tend to produce a more favourable trial outcome.[16] Had Mike Hack been able to hire Percy Anderson, and compensate him adequately for his time, it is very likely that he would have received a more effective defence.

Formal equality under the law is one thing, equal access to the benefit of the law quite another. Canadian women learned this lesson following the 1988 Supreme Court decision in *R. v. Morgentaler* that struck down the previous criminal legislation regulating abortion.[17] Once Parliament had failed a year later to pass new legislation, there was no longer any legal barrier to women with unwanted pregnancies who sought terminations. (At least no barrier in criminal law; as a medical service, abortion could be, and was, subject to provincial health regulations.) However, what women soon discovered was that the mere absence of this legal barrier – however important that might be – did not ensure effective access to the service for all who wanted it.

For one thing, the provision of abortion services rolled out very unevenly across the country. Some provinces – especially Ontario and Quebec – moved quickly to ensure that abortions would be performed both in hospitals and in freestanding clinics. Others dragged their feet. For a long time, there was no facility in Prince Edward Island that provided the service, and even now there is only one provider on the island, who will not offer an abortion later than twelve weeks into pregnancy. New Brunswick, on the other hand, allows second-trimester abortions but will pay for an abortion out of public funds only when it is done in a hospital. Women seeking an abortion in one of the province's two clinics have had to cover the cost of the procedure themselves.[18]

In addition to this patchwork of provincial policies, rural women in every province continue to find timely access to abortion more difficult than their urban counterparts. This rural–urban disparity is especially pronounced in the prairie provinces, where abortion providers are clustered in the larger cities, with few – if any – facilities available in the hinterland. For low-income rural women, seeking an abortion also means having to pay for travel expenses out of pocket (bus tickets, plane tickets, gas, hotel rooms, etc.). Travelling to the city for a procedure may require taking time off work, planning and paying for child care, elder care, and/or pet care, and buying food to bring on the trip. Many abortion providers require an escort, in which case, a family member or friend must also pay out of pocket to travel. Some women may be unable to cover those expenses and may have to delay their procedure to raise the funds. Delaying an abortion can mean exceeding the gestational limit in their province, which then entails having to travel even farther.

All women with unwanted pregnancies have an equal right to an abortion, but women who are poor and rural do not have equal access to one. In similar fashion, Mike Hack enjoyed formal equality under the law. Neither the homicide legislation in the *Criminal Code* nor the rules of criminal procedure discriminated against him on the basis of his socioeconomic status or geographical location. However, as poor and rural, he did not have equal access to justice. Someone with Hack's disabilities who committed an equivalent offence but was affluent and urban would be equally liable to apprehension, arrest, charge, indictment, and trial. But they would not be equally liable to conviction, since they would be able to afford competent and locally available counsel who would be qualified and motivated to mount a more effective defence on their behalf. And if convicted, they would not be equally liable to execution, since the same counsel could almost certainly manage a more effective application for commutation of their sentence.

Mike Hack had no greater chance in his clemency application than he had at trial. As commentators on the capital case review process have noted, reasons were never provided to support decisions for or against clemency, and the process did not seem to be guided by any evident rules.[19] For its part, the Joint Parliamentary Committee seemed not to be troubled by the absence of any stated rules or criteria:

> Since each case is judged on its own merits, the practice governing remission cannot be reduced to a statement of settled principles. The decision in many cases necessitates a review of varying circumstances and, not infrequently, the weighing of conflicting considerations. It would defeat the purpose of the exercise of the prerogative of mercy to attempt to codify the instances in which it might be invoked.[20]

As a result, we are left to guess at the considerations that weighed most heavily in these decisions. One educated guess, based on anecdotal evidence, is that the outcome of the review process was influenced by public opinion. Unlike judges and jurors, the members of Cabinet making life and death decisions about convicted murderers were elected politicians who had good reason to listen to the voice of the public. Just how influential that voice could be is nicely illustrated by the case of Angelina Napolitano, a twenty-eight-year-old Italian immigrant who, in Sault Ste Marie in 1911, killed her husband with an axe while he was sleeping. Napolitana was arrested immediately, convicted of murder, and duly sentenced to death. That sentence was never carried out, primarily because of the massive public outcry in her favour:

In Canada and elsewhere, religious people, feminists, radicals, and others participated in letter-writing and petition-signing campaigns. Within weeks of the trial, tens of thousands of men and women had denounced the Canadian criminal justice system for condemning Napolitano to death and called upon the federal government to commute the sentence to life imprisonment. Some demanded a full pardon for the convicted murderess. Women's organizations in Canada, the United States, and Britain submitted hundreds of letters and "monster petitions" bearing thousands of signatures.[21]

Napolitana's death sentence was duly commuted to life imprisonment, and she was ultimately freed after serving eleven years in the Kingston Prison for Women.[22]

By contrast, support for clemency for Mike Hack amounted, as we have seen, to five affidavits, two letters from counsel, and a petition with seventy-eight signatures. This was never going to be sufficient to sway Michael Gallagher or Ernest Lapointe or Cabinet to look past the trial judge's report of the case or reconsider their initial conclusions about it. Hack's murder of George Edey never achieved widespread publicity. His arrest, preliminary hearing, trial, and execution were reported in Saskatchewan newspapers from Melville and Yorkton to Regina and Saskatoon, but only as relatively minor news stories and not at all outside the province. At no time did there seem to be widespread public interest in this mundane killing of one farmer by another, near this obscure little village.

Nor were there extenuating circumstances likely to elicit public sympathy for the offender. Public interest, even in murder, requires something to feed on, and the Napolitano case provided plenty of nourishment. Begin with the fact that the perpetrator was a woman. Then there was the means of the murder: a violent attack with an axe rather than the poison usually preferred by homicidal women. That the victim was Angelina's husband was not unusual: most victims of murders committed by women were family members (usually husbands or children). But it was the circumstances of the crime that attracted the most attention as well as sympathy. Angelina was a mother of four and pregnant with another child. Her husband had been physically violent towards her, including an attack in which he stabbed her nine times with a pocket knife, and had threatened to kill her. Worse, at least in the eyes of many, he had pressured her to prostitute herself to augment the family finances (which she had refused to do). These factors both lent a lurid air to the whole affair and enabled her to position herself, and to be positioned by her supporters, as a wronged and abused woman desperately trying to protect her virtue. Though Mike Hack's murder of George Edey was equally violent – he clubbed him to death, after all – it had none of these further ingredients to galvanize public sympathy for the perpetrator.

In the absence of reasons given for Cabinet decisions for or against clemency, the only way to discern overall patterns in the decision-making process is to associate outcomes with other known features of the cases. Unsurprisingly, one of these features is a recommendation for mercy from either the trial judge or the jury. In the thirty-year period from 1920 to 1949, some 597 defendants were convicted and sentenced to death. Recommendations for mercy were made in 135 of these cases, 51 per cent of which resulted in commutation. In the remaining 462 cases with no recommendation, only 19 per cent of sentences were commuted.[23] As we have seen, Justice Maclean made no such recommendation – quite the contrary – and neither did the jury. One party or the other might have been better disposed to recommend mercy had Percy Anderson adduced evidence of Mike Hack's mental condition at trial. Even if an insanity defence had failed, the evidence on the table might have persuaded either judge or jury that his cognitive deficiency constituted grounds for clemency.

In search of other patterns in the decisions, Kenneth Avio conducted a regression analysis of 440 capital cases considered by Cabinet between 1926 and 1957 (including Mike Hack's) to identify factors that increased the probability of denial of clemency, and therefore of execution.[24] Avio divided these factors into two groups. Some he deemed principled in virtue of their having some degree of legal status as mitigating or aggravating circumstances in the commission of the offence. They included a previous record of violence on the part of the offender, whether the victim was a police officer, whether there were multiple victims, whether the violence was provoked by the victim, whether the offender was under the influence of another person, whether the murder was brutal, whether it was premeditated, whether it was committed in the course of a felony, whether the offender confessed and cooperated with the authorities, and whether the offender attempted suicide. (This last factor was apparently taken to indicate presence (or absence) of remorse.) In terms of these factors, the balance for Mike Hack tips towards denial of clemency. On the one hand, he had no previous record of violence (though he had been arrested twice for theft) and his sole victim was not a police officer. On the other hand, his murder of George Edey was unprovoked, brutal, premeditated, and committed in the course of a robbery. Further, Hack was not acting under anyone else's influence, he did not confess (or even seem to understand the seriousness of his action), and he did not attempt suicide.

There was, however, one other mitigating factor on Avio's list that merits special consideration: whether the offender was suffering from a mental disease or defect. As we know, Mike Hack did have a mental defect, but evidence of it was not adduced at trial. Once again, the absence of that evidence is significant, even crucial. Had the Remission Service and Cabinet been convinced of his cognitive deficiency, that could have made the difference between clemency and execution. Hack's mental condition therefore should have been a factor in his favour, though it proved not to be. But it may also have worked against him, especially when compounded by his deafness. As we have seen, Hack was an inconvenient client for Percy Anderson, by virtue of his poverty and rural location. His disabilities made him more inconvenient still, since Anderson could not easily communicate with him and evidently had considerable difficulty getting him to appreciate the seriousness of his situation. Kent Roach has shown how cognitive impairment can be a risk factor for wrongful conviction, by increasing the likelihood that the accused will accept a guilty plea to a lesser offence, despite being factually innocent.[25] Hack's dual impairments may have had a similar effect, by making him more likely to be neglected by his defence counsel.

The attributes of the offender that Avio considered extra-legal were age, gender, socioeconomic status, race, and ethnicity. Of these, we can disregard race, since both Mike Hack and George Edey were white. Hack's German/Ukrainian ethnicity was considered earlier as a possible factor in swaying the jury towards conviction, but dismissed there for absence of supporting evidence. But now the question is whether it might have played any role in the outcome of the clemency application. While his ethnicity might not have mattered to the jurors, it might have been more salient for Donald Maclean, or Herbert Sampson, or Michael Gallagher, or Ernest Lapointe. Avio's analysis showed that Eastern European offenders (including Galicians) had a significantly higher likelihood of denial of clemency than Anglo-Canadians. Whether or not the strong anti-Ukrainian sentiment prevalent in the country at that time played any role with the jury, it might well have had an influence on the major players in the clemency process.[26]

We are left, then, with three extra-legal factors: age, gender, and socioeconomic status. Of these, "the single most significant factor to shape the likelihood or unlikelihood of execution was gender."[27] The data on gender are somewhat compromised by the relatively small sample size of female murderers. Women just do not commit murder as frequently as men. From 1920 to 1949, 573 men were sentenced to death for murder, compared with 24 women.[28] During that same period, 456 male cases were considered for clemency by Cabinet, as opposed to 14 female. (The remaining cases were disposed in other ways: appeal to a higher court, new trial ordered by minister, suicide of offender, etc.) The clemency rate for men was 32.5 per cent, for women 64.3 per cent.

This bias against hanging women held firm even when their crimes were particularly grotesque. In two notorious cases, the victims were children (or stepchildren). The strangest was the case of Minnie McGee in Prince Edward Island. During the first four months of 1912, all eight of the McGee children died, apparently of natural causes. For the first two, an infant and a toddler, the cause of death was pneumonia. The symptoms of the remaining six children were more puzzling and more suspicious: "their heads, chests, and stomachs pained them; they vomited; their skins paled, pulses weakened, and their lips became bluish; they grew unable to walk; and, ultimately, their hearts failed."[29] Following an autopsy on one of the children, it was determined that the cause of death was phosphorous poisoning. McGee was charged with the murder of her child.

It was well known at the time that white phosphorous was a potent poison; the contents of one matchbox were sufficient to kill a person. Long-term exposure to the chemical by workers in match factories could lead to an affliction called "phossy jaw": an erosion of gum and bone mass whose only treatment was removal of the lower jaw. For that reason, the use of the chemical in the manufacture of matches was banned in the Berne Convention of 1906. This agreement, however, required each signatory nation to pass its own enforcing legislation, and Canada did not do so until 1914, spurred in part by the notoriety of Minnie McGee's crime.

Despite doubts about McGee's mental state on the part of defence counsel – and on her part as well – a defence of insanity was not attempted at the trial. Minnie was convicted of murder after only a half-hour's deliberation by the jury. Before sentencing, she confessed that she had soaked matches in weak tea and sugar water, which she then fed to the children. In her confession, she said that in January of that year her head "went all astray" and then got worse in the months to follow.[30] She also said that she had intended to kill herself in the same way. Despite the fact that the jury had heard no evidence of insanity, it nonetheless recommended mercy, evidently believing that she must somehow have been deranged. Following the trial, the local community mounted a campaign for clemency on the same basis. The memo prepared for the minister of justice noted that "the woman is somewhat defective mentally, but nevertheless not irresponsible in the legal sense."[31] Her sentence was duly commuted to life imprisonment. She died in Falconwood Hospital, PEI, in January 1953.

Equally lurid was the crime of Anne-Marie Houde, who in April 1920 was tried in Quebec City for the murder of her ten-year-old stepdaughter, Aurore, who became known as *"l'enfant martyre."*[32] Houde and her husband, Télesphore Gagnon, lived in a blended household, with three of his children, one of hers, and one offspring of the marriage. The local doctor who performed the autopsy on Aurore's body identified "dozens of grotesque injuries to the child's legs, face, feet, and virtually every other part of her body, speculating that some of them could have been caused by blows with a whip or a narrow piece of wood."[33] Because the death was considered suspicious, both Anne-Marie and Télesphore were committed for trial, she for murder and he for manslaughter. Evidence given at Houde's trial, in part by her own eleven-year-old son, showed that she "had not only beaten the child with such instruments as whips and axe handles, but had restrained her with ropes and deliberately burned her with a poker, heated red-hot on a wood stove."[34] Houde's defence counsel attempted a plea of insanity, based in part on the fact that she was four months pregnant at the time of Aurore's death, but the trial judge virtually instructed the jury to disregard it, and Houde was duly convicted of murder. Her husband was convicted of manslaughter in a separate trial, for his part in the beating and death of the child. Houde's hanging was scheduled for October 1920, so that there would be time beforehand for her pregnancy to come to term. She gave birth to twins, a boy and a girl, in the Quebec City jail in July.

Despite the horrific nature of the crime, the outpouring of public sympathy for the "martyred" child, and the fact that Houde seemed the very paradigm of the wicked stepmother, a clemency campaign was organized on her behalf by the Montreal-based Canadian Prisoners' Welfare Association, the group of which Robert Bickerdike had been one of the founders. The basis of the campaign was not so much sympathy for Houde, or a claim of insanity on her behalf, but rather that a nursing mother should not be separated from her newborn babies. Her sentence was commuted, and she spent most of the rest of her life in Kingston Penitentiary. She was released in July 1935 but died of cancer less than a year later.

The evidence of Cabinet's reluctance to hang women is quite conclusive. Avio also found that young offenders, between twenty-one and fifty-five years of age, were at increased risk of execution.[35] On the other hand, the evidence of bias against murderers of lower socioeconomic status was weaker. In the absence of other socioeconomic information about offenders, occupation had to serve as a surrogate. Avio found that, other factors being equal, those classified as "labourer" were slightly less likely to have their sentence commuted than those in all other occupational categories.

Of the various factors bearing on commutation that Avio examined, those that he classified as principled were, at least theoretically, within the control of the offender. Mike Hack, therefore, could have chosen not to commit an unprovoked, brutal, and premeditated murder to rob George Edey of his horses and, once having done so, he could have expressed some remorse for his actions. To that extent, he was the architect of his own fate. However, he had no control over being young, male, ethnic, and poor. As Carolyn Strange has put it, "patterns of severity were generally disfavourable to the poor, to men, and to those from identifiable racial and ethnic groups."[36] Hold every other circumstance of the crime constant, and those features all increased the likelihood that he would hang for it.

Mike Hack ticked virtually all the boxes for the murder suspect most likely to be both convicted and executed for their crime: age (young), gender (male), ethnicity (German), occupation (labourer), socioeconomic condition (poor), geographical location (rural), and disability (deaf and intellectually impaired). When all these factors are taken into consideration, it is hard not to conclude that his ultimate fate was effectively sealed on that night in early May when George Edey came up to the hayloft to feed his horses.

# Notes

**Preface**

1 Len W. Sumner, *Raw Prairie to Grain Elevators: The Chronicles of a Pioneer Community Duff, Saskatchewan* (Toronto: Dundurn Press, 1980).
2 Len W. Sumner, *Pheasant Forks: History 1882–1905* (Toronto: Self-published, 1982).

**1. Settlement**

1 *Saskatchewan Gazette*, November 26, 2021, 3630–3.
2 Sumner, *Pheasant Forks*, 8.
3 Alan B. Anderson, *Settling Saskatchewan* (Regina: University of Regina Press, 2013), ch. 2; John H. Archer, *Saskatchewan: A History* (Saskatoon: Western Producer Prairie Books, 1980), ch. 1.
4 An Act Respecting the Public Lands of the Dominion, SC 1872, c. 23.
5 For fuller information on the DLS, see Robert B. McKercher and Bertram Wolfe, *Understanding Western Canada's Dominion Land Survey System* (Saskatoon: University of Saskatchewan, 1986).
6 https://www.cbc.ca/news/canada/saskatoon/saskatchewan-homesteaders-had-difficult-road-to-success-1.3609347, accessed 18 November 2022.
7 Anderson, *Settling Saskatchewan*.
8 For an account of the Company's activities and its success in establishing a settlement near the Pheasant Creek, see Sumner, *Pheasant Forks*; Anderson, *Settling Saskatchewan*. Pheasant Hills/Creek/Forks: all so named by English settlers for the resemblance of prairie chickens and partridge to pheasants back home.
9 Anderson, *Settling Saskatchewan*. From 1908, settlers had either to be, or declare an intention to be, a British subject.

10 The history of German immigration to the province is comprehensively related in Anderson, *Settling Saskatchewan*. For German settlement in the Pheasant Hills area, see ibid., 102–4.

## 2. May 1928

1 "The Passing of the S.P.P.," *Public Service Monthly*, June 1928.
2 Details concerning the course of that investigation, and the information obtained from it, are drawn from Crime Reports by Constable William Bannerman, SPP (12 May 1928), Detective Sergeant Charles Dunnett, SPP (14 May), Constable James W. Watts, SPP (16 May), Corporal J. G. Metcalfe, RCMP (19 May), and Corporal J. Laight, SPP (20 & 25 May).
3 Site W2–22–9-W2.
4 Letter of Hector and Janet Kenridge to Len W. Sumner, 1 September 1982.
5 Crime Report, Constable James W. Watts, p. 2.
6 R.S.S. 1920, c. 65, s. 4.
7 For her interesting story, see Myrna L. Petersen, *The Pathological Casebook of Dr. Frances McGill* (Regina: Ideation Entertainment, 2005).
8 Crime Report, Constable Bannerman. Several typos in Dr. Findlay's testimony have been corrected.
9 Ibid.
10 David M. Paciocco, "A Voyage of Discovery: Examining the Precarious Condition of the Preliminary Inquiry," *Criminal Law Quarterly* 48, no. 2 (2003): 151n1; *Criminal Code*, 55–56 Victoria, 1892, c. 29 [henceforth: 1892 *Code*], Part XLV.
11 In the late nineteenth century, this process was also known as committal proceedings; see, e.g., Robert J. Sharpe, *The Lazier Murder: Prince Edward County, 1884* (Toronto: University of Toronto Press, 2011), ch. 6.
12 See Paciocco, "A Voyage of Discovery," 151; Cheryl Marie Webster, "Why Re-Open the Debate on the Preliminary Inquiry? Some Preliminary Empirical Observations," *Canadian Journal of Criminology and Criminal Justice* 55, no. 4 (2013); Steve Coughlan, *Criminal Procedure*, 4th ed. (Toronto: Irwin Law, 2020), ch. 9.
13 *R. v. Jordan*, 2016 SCC 27, 1.
14 *R. v. Stinchcombe*, [1991] 3 S.C.R. 326.
15 *R. v. S.J.L.* [2009] 1 S.C.R. 426, at para 23.
16 Melville *Advance*, 24 May 1928.

## 3. How Justice Can Miscarry

1 *Report of the Kaufman Commission on Proceedings Involving Guy Paul Morin* (1998).
2 See the *Royal Commission on the Donald Marshall, Jr. Prosecution: Digest of Findings and Recommendations* (1989). See also Michael Harris, *Justice Denied: The Law Versus Donald Marshall* (Toronto: Macmillan of Canada, 1986).

Notes to pages 30–3

3 For a fuller list, see the Innocence Canada website: "Exonerations," accessed 30 November 2022, https://www.innocencecanada.com/exonerations/.
4 "What We Do, History & Mission," Innocence Canada, accessed 30 November 2022, https://www.innocencecanada.com/about-us/.
5 For more on the story of Steven Truscott, see Julian Sher, *"Until You Are Dead": Steven Truscott's Long Ride into History* (Toronto: Seal Books, 2008).
6 Isabel LeBordais, *The Trial of Steven Truscott* (Toronto: McClelland and Stewart, 1966).
7 *Reference re: Steven Murray Truscott*, [1967] S.C.R. 309. I owe this information to one of the anonymous reviewers of this book.
8 *Truscott (Re)*, 2007 ONCA 575, at para 787.
9 *Truscott (Re)*, at para 264.
10 Michael Naughton, "Redefining Miscarriages of Justice: A Revived Human-Rights Approach to Unearth Subjugated Discourses of Wrongful Criminal Conviction," *British Journal of Criminology* 45, no. 2 (2005); Michael Naughton, *Rethinking Miscarriages of Justice: Beyond the Tip of the Iceberg* (Houndmills: Palgrave Macmillan, 2007), 15ff.; Kent Roach, "Exonerating the Wrongfully Convicted: Do We Need Innocence Hearings?" in *Honouring Social Justice: Honouring Dianne Martin*, ed. Margaret E. Beare (Toronto: University of Toronto Press, 2008); Kent Roach, "Wrongful Convictions in Canada," *University of Cincinnati Law Review* 80, no. 4 (2012): 1470–2; Kent Roach, "Defining Miscarriages of Justice in the Context of Post-911 Counter-Terrorism," in *Counter-Terrorism, Constitutionalism, and Miscarriages of Justice: A Festschrift for Professor Clive Walker*, ed. Genevieve Lennon, Colin King, and Carole McCartney (Oxford: Hart Publishing, 2018).
11 *Re Phillion*, 2009 ONCA 202 (Can.). The court did order a new trial in this case, but the Crown did not proceed because, after such a long time, there was little likelihood of securing a conviction. I owe this information to one of the anonymous reviewers of this book.
12 As is suggested by Carole McCartney and Clive Walker, "Criminal Justice and Miscarriages of Justice in England and Wales," in *Wrongful Conviction: International Perspectives on Miscarriages of Justice*, ed. C. Ronald Huff and Martin Killias (Philadelphia: Temple University Press, 2008). See also Roach, "Defining Miscarriages."
13 The definition of a wrongful conviction in the Canadian Registry of Wrongful Convictions does not require proof of factual innocence: https://www.wrongfulconvictions.ca/, accessed 29 April 2023. In this, it followed the lead of the National Registry of Exonerations in the United States: https://www.law.umich.edu/special/exoneration/Pages/about.aspx, accessed 5 December 2022. See Kent Roach, *Wrongfully Convicted: Guilty Pleas, Imagined Crimes, and What Canada Must Do to Safeguard Justice* (New York: Simon & Schuster, 2023), xxii–xxiv.

14 David Alan D. Asper, "Wrongful Convictions in Canada and Defence Counsel: It's Time for Mandatory Professional Education and Competency Safeguards," Masters thesis (Toronto: University of Toronto, 2007), 19ff.

### 4. October 1928

1 Melanie Cole, "The Brutal Murder of Florence Beatty," *Melanie Cole*, 14 March 2023, https://melaniecole.com/2023/03/14/the-brutal-murder-of-florence-beatty/.
2 Petersen, *Pathological Casebook*, 107.
3 Regina *Morning Leader*, 4 October 1928.
4 Regina *Morning Leader*, 5 October 1928.
5 Marjorie Freeman Campbell, *A Century of Crime: The Development of Crime Detection Methods in Canada* (Toronto: McClelland & Stewart, 1970), 124, 170–2.
6 Herbert J. Walter, "Rex Vs. Mike Hack: Handwriting in a Murder Trial in Western Canada," *American Journal of Police Science* 3, no. 1 (1932).
7 *Criminal Code*, R.S., 1927, c. 146 [henceforth: 1927 *Code*], s. 259 (a)(b). All further references will be to this version of the *Code*, unless otherwise indicated, because it was the one in force at the time of Mike Hack's trial.
8 The *Code* (s. 262) simply defined manslaughter as "Culpable homicide, not amounting to murder."
9 The death penalty remained in effect after 1976 for some offences under the *National Defence Act*, but was later abolished for those as well.
10 David B. Chandler, *Capital Punishment in Canada: A Sociological Study of Repressive Law* (Toronto: McClelland and Stewart, 1976), ch. 2.
11 "Robert Bickerdike," *Dictionary of Canadian Biography*, accessed 1 January 2023, http://www.biographi.ca/en/bio/bickerdike_robert_15E.html.
12 An Act to amend the Criminal Code (Capital Murder), 9–10 Eliz. II, c. 44.
13 Regina *Morning Leader*, 6 October 1928.

### 5. The Roads Not Taken

1 *R. v. Bradley*, 2015 ONCA 738 (CanLII), per Watt JA, at para 184.
2 Sharpe, *Lazier Murder*.
3 Sharpe, *Lazier Murder*, 5.
4 Sharpe, *Lazier Murder*, ch. 4.
5 Jaroslav Petryshyn and L. Dzubak, *Peasants in the Promised Land: Canada and the Ukrainians, 1891–1914* (Toronto: James Lorimer, 1985), ch. 7.
6 Crime Report, 21 October 1928.
7 Average duration of capital trials culminating in convictions in 1928 was 2.5 days and in 1958 was 5.4 days.

8 Crime Report, 21 October 1928.
9 Sharpe, *Lazier Murder*, 83–6.
10 Coughlan, *Criminal Procedure*, 524.
11 I owe this creative suggestion to one of the anonymous reviewers of this book.
12 See Andrew Simester, *Fundamentals of Criminal Law: Responsibility, Culpability, and Wrongdoing* (Oxford: Oxford University Press, 2021), ch. 17.
13 Simester calls these defences of irresponsibility. But since their point is to show that the agent lacked the capacity for moral reasoning at the time of the offence, "non-responsibility" seems more apt.
14 Charles Patrick Ewing, *Murder, Madness, and the Law* (Oxford: Oxford University Press, 2008), xxvii–xxviii.
15 For more information on the case, see Richard Moran, *Knowing Right from Wrong: The Insanity Defense of Daniel M'Naghten* (New York: Free Press, 1981). In a later work (Richard Moran, "McNaughtan [McNaghten], Daniel," in *Oxford Dictionary of National Biography* [Oxford: Oxford University Press, 2004]), Moran advances the (unproven) hypothesis that M'Naghten was actually hired to assassinate the prime minister, and subsequently feigned insanity to escape legal liability and the gallows.
16 *M'Naghten's Case* [1843] All ER Rep 229 at 230.
17 M'Naghten Rules (1843) 4 St.Tr. (N.S.) 847.
18 The smallpox vaccine was first introduced by Edward Jenner in 1796.
19 Renumbered, but unchanged, as s. 19(1) in the 1927 *Code*. For a very useful overview of the insanity defence in Canadian criminal law, see Kent Roach, *Criminal Law*, 7th ed. (Toronto: Irwin Law, 2018), ch. 8.
20 1927 *Code*, s. 19(3).
21 See Simon N. Verdun-Jones, "The Evolution of the Defences of Insanity and Automatism in Canada from 1843 to 1979: A Saga of Reluctance to Sever the Umbilical Cord to the Mother Country?" *University of British Columbia Law Review* 14, no. 1 (1979): 20ff.
22 *Cooper v. R.*, [1980] 1 S.C.R. 1149, at 1159. Citing the definition in *Cooper*, Lofchik J. of the Ontario Supreme Court later concluded that "mental retardation" qualifies as a "disease of the mind": *R. v. M.S.R.*, 1996 CanLII 8294 (ON SC), at para 13. This would seem to erase the distinction between "disease of the mind" and "natural imbecility."
23 Adelle Purdham, "One commonly used word we need to release into the abyss of history," *Toronto Star*, 24 February 2024.
24 James W. Trent, *Inventing the Feeble Mind: A History of Intellectual Disability in the United States* (New York: Oxford University Press, 2017), ch. 5.
25 Douglas K. Detterman, Lynne T. Gabriel, and Joanne M. Ruthsatz, "Intelligence and Mental Retardation," in *Handbook of Intelligence*, ed. Robert J. Sternberg (Cambridge: Cambridge University Press, 2000).
26 See, for instance, Verdun-Jones, "Evolution of Insanity," 26ff.

27 Roach, *Criminal Law*, 329–31.
28 *R. v. Barnier*, [1980] 1 S.C.R. 1124, at 1125.
29 Verdun-Jones, "Evolution of Insanity," 30ff; Simon N. Verdun-Jones, "The Insanity Defence in Canada: Setting a New Course," *International Journal of Law and Psychiatry* 17, no. 2 (1994): 185ff; Roach, *Criminal Law*, 331–4.
30 Verdun-Jones, "Evolution of Insanity," 30.
31 Verdun-Jones, "Evolution of Insanity," 31–2. As did the Supreme Court of Canada in *Schwartz v. R.*, [1977] 1 S.C.R. 673.
32 Verdun-Jones, "Evolution of Insanity," 33.
33 *R. v. Chaulk* [1990] 3 S.C.R. 1303, at 1354.
34 Ibid., at 1356.
35 Ibid., at 1357 (emphasis added).
36 *R. v. Minassian*, 2021 ONSC 1258.
37 Ibid., at para 58 (emphasis added).
38 *R. v. Oommen*, [1994] 2 S.C.R. 507, 30 CR (4th) 195.
39 *Minassian*, at para 204.
40 Ibid., at para 231.
41 Ibid., at para 255.
42 Martin L. Friedland, *The Case of Valentine Shortis: A True Story of Crime and Politics in Canada* (Toronto: University of Toronto Press, 1986).
43 Now the Centre for Addiction and Mental Health (CAMH).
44 Friedland, *Valentine Shortis*, 109–10.
45 Verdun-Jones, "Evolution of Insanity," 26, 33.
46 *R. v. Cracknell* [1931] OR 634, at 637.
47 *R. v. Jeanotte* [1932] 2 WWR 283.
48 1927 *Code*, s. 966.
49 *Criminal Code*, R.S.C., 1985, c. C-46 [henceforth: 1985 *Code*], s. 2.
50 1927 *Code*, s. 967(5).
51 Erica Dyck and Alex Deighton, *Managing Madness: Weyburn Mental Hospital and the Transformation of Psychiatric Care in Canada* (Winnipeg: University of Manitoba Press, 2017), chs. 1 & 2.
52 Dyck and Deighton, *Managing Madness*, 55ff; Alex Deighton, "The Last Asylum: Experiencing the Weyburn Mental Hospital, 1921–1939," Masters thesis (University of Saskatchewan, 2016), ch. 2.
53 Deighton, "The Last Asylum," 32.

### 6. "He was German, he was deaf and a little simple"

1 Letter of Pastor Don Reimer to Len W. Sumner, 8 October 1982.
2 Affidavit of Dora Hack, 28 November 1928.
3 Affidavit of Fred Hack, 28 November 1928.

4 Affidavit of Walter Krahn, 1 December 1928.
5 Not meaning what it does today, but rather "odd" or "weird."
6 Affidavit of Jacob Niebergall, 3 December 1928.
7 Affidavits of Jacob Niebergall and Philip Armbruster, 4 December 1928.
8 Andrew Solomon, *Far from the Tree: Parents, Children, and the Search for Identity* (New York: Scribner, 2012), 2.
9 Solomon, *Far from the Tree*, ch. 7.
10 Last will and testament of Mathias Hack, 14 August 1925.
11 Affidavit of Jacob Niebergall, 3 December 1928.
12 Letter of Jack Orbin and Fran Smulan to Len W. Sumner, 28 September 1983.
13 Solomon, *Far from the Tree*, ch. 10.
14 Solomon, *Far from the Tree*, ch. 2.
15 Affidavit of Fred Hack, 28 November 1928.
16 Letter of Rita Csada to Len W. Sumner, 26 April 1982.
17 Letter of Herbert Sampson to deputy attorney general, 4 January 1929.
18 *R. v. G.D.B.*, [2000] 1 S.C.R. 520, at paras 24–5.
19 Some think worse: for example, Dale E. Ives, "The 'Canadian' Approach to Ineffective Assistance of Counsel Claims," *Brandeis Law Journal* 42, no. 2 (2003–4).
20 *Strickland v. Washington*, 466 U.S. 668 (1984). There is an important similarity between this case and the trial of Mike Hack. In *Strickland*, the accused was sentenced to death on three capital murder charges. One of the claims against defence counsel was that he had failed to request a psychiatric examination of his client, whose result could have led the court to impose a lesser sentence.
21 Ibid., at 689.
22 Ibid., at 687.
23 *G.D.B.*, at para 27.
24 Ibid., at para 26.
25 Ibid., at para 28.
26 David M. Tanovich, "Further Developments on Claims of Ineffectiveness of Counsel," *Criminal Reports (4th)* 34, no. 32 (1995); Ives, "The 'Canadian' Approach"; Dale E. Ives, "Failure to Interview a Potential Defence Witness as the Basis for an Ineffective Assistance of Counsel Claim," *Criminal Law Quarterly* 53, no. 4 (2007–8).
27 "If trial counsel did not know of a potential witness' existence, but ought reasonably to have known about it, appeal courts should conclude that trial counsel acted incompetently." Ives, "Failure to Interview," p. 509.
28 In the United States, claims of ineffective assistance have succeeded, using the *Strickland* tests, where counsel failed to introduce expert evidence,

including evidence of the accused's insanity. (David M. Tanovich, "Charting the Constitutional Right of Effective Assistance of Counsel in Canada," *Criminal Law Quarterly* 36, no. 4 [1994]: p. 421.)
29 *Strickland*, at 694.
30 Ives, "Failure to Interview," p. 524.
31 Letter of Herbert E. Sampson to deputy attorney general, 4 January 1929.
32 Letter of Herbert E. Sampson to deputy attorney general, 4 January 1929.
33 Martin L. Friedland, *A Century of Criminal Justice: Perspectives on the Development of Canadian Law* (Toronto: Carswell Legal Publications, 1984), 242–5.
34 Michael Boudreau, "'He Was Always a Mental Defective': Psychiatric Conversations and the Execution of Bennie Swim in New Brunswick, 1922," *Journal of New Brunswick Studies* 12, no. 1 (2020).
35 Swim actually had the distinction of being hanged twice: Ken Leyton-Brown, *The Practice of Execution in Canada* (Vancouver: UBC Press, 2010), 97.
36 Elaine Burton, "The Last Hanging at the Old Port Arthur Jail: A Case Study in Capital Punishment," Course paper (University of Toronto, 1994).
37 Burton, "Last Hanging," 24.
38 Burton, "Last Hanging," 28.
39 Burton, "Last Hanging," 25.
40 Kimberley White, *Negotiating Responsibility: Law, Murder, and States of Mind* (Vancouver: UBC Press, 2008), 18.
41 Letter of Percy Anderson to Ernest Lapointe, 24 November 1928.
42 https://psycnet.apa.org/doiLanding?doi=10.1037%2Ft02322-000, accessed 27 June 2023.
43 McCay Vernon and Katrina Miller, "Obstacles Faced by Deaf People in the Criminal Justice System," *American Annals of the Deaf* 150, no. 3 (2005); Fiona Davidson, et al., "Assessing Fitness for Trial for Deaf Defendants," *Psychiatry, Psychology and Law* 22, no. 1 (2015).
44 McCay Vernon, Annie G. Steinberg, and Louise A. Montoya, "Deaf Murderers: Clinical and Forensic Issues," *Behavioral Sciences and the Law* 17, no. 4 (1999).
45 Letter from Herbert Sampson to deputy attorney general, 4 January 1929.
46 Judge's Report, 5 December 1928.
47 Regina *Morning Leader*, 5 October 1928.
48 Letter of William Elliott to Percy Anderson, 26 December 1928.
49 Appeal of a murder conviction became automatic in 1961, following the recommendation of the 1956 joint parliamentary committee (Joint Committee of the Senate and House of Commons, *Final Report on Capital Punishment* [Ottawa: Queen's Printer, 1956], para 83).

50 During the 1920s, of 190 murder convictions in Canada, 28 (15 per cent) were successfully appealed. (Joint Committee of the Senate and House of Commons, "Final Report," para 18).
51 1927 *Code*, s. 1014(2).
52 1927 *Code*, s. 1014(1)(c).
53 For ineffective assistance as a cause of wrongful conviction, and therefore a ground of appeal, see Roach, "Wrongful Convictions," 1512–13.
54 G. Arthur Martin, "The Role and Responsibility of the Defence Advocate," *Criminal Law Quarterly* 12, no. 4 (1970). See also Michel Proulx and David Layton, *Ethics and Canadian Criminal Law* (Toronto: Irwin Law, 2001), 101ff.
55 1927 *Code*, s. 1022.
56 This authority was rarely exercised: from 1892 to 1955, the minister ordered a new trial in only nine capital cases (Carolyn Strange, "The Lottery of Death: Capital Punishment, 1867–1976," *Manitoba Law Journal* 23 [1995]: 598). However, in at least one instance, it led to an acquittal on grounds of insanity (Joint Committee of the Senate and House of Commons, "Final Report," para 10).
57 Carolyn Strange, "Discretionary Justice: Political Culture and the Death Penalty in New South Wales and Ontario, 1890–1920," in *Qualities of Mercy: Justice, Punishment, and Discretion*, ed. Carolyn Strange (Vancouver: UBC Press, 1996), 148.
58 I am grateful to Jim Phillips for suggesting this possibility.

## 7. The Royal Prerogative of Mercy

1 Trial transcript.
2 Ss. 1076, 1077.
3 Joint Committee of the Senate and House of Commons, "*Final Report*," para 20.
4 All the cases can be found in Lorraine Gadoury and Antonio Lechasseur, *Persons Sentenced to Death in Canada, 1867–1976: An Inventory of Case Files in the Fonds of the Department of Justice* (Ottawa: National Archives of Canada, 1994).
5 Joint Committee of the Senate and House of Commons, "*Final Report*," para 19.
6 Thomas M. Sheehan, "Administrative Review and Capital Punishment: The Canadian Concept," *American Journal of Correction* 27, no. 1 (1965); Strange, "Lottery of Death," 597–9; Carolyn Strange, *The Death Penalty and Sex Murder in Canadian History* (Toronto: University of Toronto Press, 2020), 6–7.
7 Strange, *Death Penalty*, 62.

140   Notes to pages 96–111

8 A similar petition, with more than 400 signatories, was presented to the minister of justice as part of the clemency appeal of George Lowder and Joseph Thomset. It was similarly unsuccessful (Sharpe, *Lazier Murder*, 131–2).
9 Alex Deighton, "The Nature of Eugenic Thought and Limits of Eugenic Practice in Interwar Saskatchewan," in *Eugenics at the Edges of Empire: New Zealand, Australia, Canada and South Africa*, ed. Diane B. Paul, John Stenhouse, and Hamish G. Spencer (Cham, Switzerland: Palgrave Macmillan, 2018).
10 Dyck and Deighton, *Managing Madness*, 16ff; Deighton, "The Last Asylum," ch. 3.
11 Dyck and Deighton, *Managing Madness*, 64. By the mid-1930s, Campbell had come to doubt both the science on which eugenics was based and the policy of segregating the mentally defective (Dyck and Deighton, *Managing Madness*, 80).
12 Dyck and Deighton, *Managing Madness*, 16–18, 73ff.
13 In 1928, the male side of the hospital was overcrowded by 44 per cent (Dyck and Deighton, *Managing Madness*, 55).
14 Dyck and Deighton, *Managing Madness*, 79.
15 Deighton, "The Last Asylum," ch. 3.
16 Joint Committee of the Senate and House of Commons, "Final Report," para 11.
17 Joint Committee of the Senate and House of Commons, "Final Report," op. cit., para 15.
18 This point was raised by one of the anonymous reviewers of this book.
19 David M. Paciocco, Palma Paciocco, and Lee Struesser, *The Law of Evidence*, 8th ed. (Toronto: Irwin Law, 2020), ch. 5.

## 8. January 1929

1 F.W. Anderson, *A Concise History of Capital Punishment in Canada* (Calgary: Frontier Publishing, 1973), chs. 6 & 7; Leyton-Brown, *Practice of Execution*, op. cit., chs. 6 & 7; Lorna Poplak, *Drop Dead: A Horrible History of Hanging in Canada* (Toronto: Dundurn, 2017), ch. 9.
2 Joint Committee of the Senate and House of Commons, "Final Report," paras 89–94.
3 Poplak, *Drop Dead*, pp. 80–1.
4 This was not the first decapitation in Ellis's career: Leyton-Brown, *Practice of Execution*, 94.
5 Regina *Morning Leader*, 17 January 1929.
6 Regina *Morning Leader*, 18 January 1929.

Notes to pages 111–19

7 Translation of copy of original manuscript letter, obtained from Saskatchewan Archives.
8 Regina *Morning Leader*, 19 January 1929. The following account of the hanging is taken from the same source.

### 9. The Bigger Picture

1 Eve Brensike Primus, "Disaggregating Ineffective Assistance of Counsel Doctrine: Four Forms of Constitutional Ineffectiveness," *Stanford Law Review* 72, no. 6 (2020).
2 Primus, "Ineffective Assistance," 1586.
3 The relative merits of the two systems are frequently debated; see Albert Currie, "Legal Aid Delivery Models in Canada: Past Experience and Future Developments," *University of British Columbia Law Review* 33, no. 2 (2000). For one study showing that "public defender [staff lawyer] offices have a better performance record than appointed counsel," see Scott Phillips, "Legal Disparities in the Capital of Capital Punishment," *Journal of Criminal Law and Criminology* 99, no. 3 (2009): 754.
4 Frederick H. Zemans, "Legal Aid and Legal Advice in Canada: An Overview of the Last Decade in Quebec, Saskatchewan and Ontario," *Osgoode Hall Law Journal* 16, no. 3 (1978): 681ff.
5 Zemans, "Legal Aid," 676ff.; Jennie Abell, "Ideology and the Emergence of Legal Aid in Saskatchewan," *Dalhousie Law Journal* 16, no. 1 (1993): 158ff.
6 John P. Nelligan, "Legal Aid in Canada: Existing Facilities," *Canadian Bar Review* 29, no. 6 (1951): 607ff.
7 Joe L. Salterio, "Fees for Defence of Indigent Persons," *Saskatchewan Bar Review and Law Society's Gazette* 14, no. 2 (1949).
8 Nelligan, "Legal Aid," 608. The same issue concerning fees was flagged in a study of murder cases in an American jurisdiction that employed the private bar system (Phillips, "Legal Disparities," 728–9, 754–5).
9 Nelligan, "Legal Aid," 608–9; Phillips, "Legal Disparities," 728–9, 754–5. In 1956, the joint parliamentary committee considering the death penalty recommended that defence counsel be paid for their services to indigent clients, and that funds also be made available for the preparation of the defence (Joint Committee of the Senate and House of Commons, "Final Report," para 80).
10 For a defence in a murder case on a similar basis, and with a similar outcome, see Friedland, *A Century of Criminal Justice*, 241.
11 Zemans, "Legal Aid," 676.
12 Garrett Wilson and Kevin Wilson, *Diefenbaker for the Defence* (Toronto: James Lorimer, 1988), 70–3.

13 Wilson and Wilson, *Diefenbaker*, ch. 6.
14 Wilson and Wilson, *Diefenbaker*, 108.
15 Ronald A. Farrell and Victoria L. Swigert, "Adjudication in Homicide: An Interpretive Analysis of the Effects of Defendant and Victim Social Characteristics," *Journal of Research in Crime and Delinquency* 23, no. 4 (1986): 357–8.
16 Victoria L. Swigert and Ronald A. Farrell, "Normal Homicides and the Law," *American Sociological Review* 42, no. 1 (1977): 27; Farrell and Swigert, "Adjudication in Homicide," 356–60.
17 *R. v. Morgentaler*, [1988] 1 S.C.R. 30.
18 The two clinics became one in February 2024, when Clinic 554 in Fredericton closed its doors "over financial pressures incurred from providing pro-bono abortion procedures to women who can't afford to pay for them out of pocket." CBC News, 31 January 2024, accessed 2 February 2024, https://www.cbc.ca/news/canada/new-brunswick/clinic-554-fredericton-abortion-1.7100433.
19 Strange, "Lottery of Death."
20 Joint Committee of the Senate and House of Commons, "Final Report," para 12.
21 Karen Dubinsky and Franca Iacovetta, "Murder, Womanly Virtue, and Motherhood: The Case of Angelina Napolitano, 1911–1922," *Canadian Historical Review* 72, no. 4 (1991): 505–6.
22 The fact that a female murderer's victim was her husband was not always sufficient for clemency: Marie Beaulne (1929), Phoebe Campbell (1871), Marie-Louise Cloutier (1937), Tommasina Teolis (1934), Elizabeth Ann Tilford (1935), Cordelia Viau (1897), and Elizabeth Workman (1873) were all hanged for the murder of their husbands (Gadoury and Lechasseur, *Persons Sentenced*).
23 Joint Committee of the Senate and House of Commons, "Final Report," Table F, p. 31.
24 Kenneth L. Avio, "The Quality of Mercy: Exercise of the Royal Prerogative in Canada," *Canadian Public Policy* 13, no. 3 (1987). See also Chandler, *Capital Punishment*; Kenneth L. Avio, "Capital Punishment in Canada: Statistical Evidence and Constitutional Issues," *Canadian Journal of Criminology* 30, no. 4 (1988).
25 Roach, *Wrongfully Convicted*, 11–15.
26 Cf. Strange, "Lottery of Death," 614–16.
27 Strange, "Lottery of Death," 607.
28 Joint Committee of the Senate and House of Commons, "Final Report," Table B, p. 29.

29 Sharon Myers, "The Apocrypha of Minnie McGee: The Murderous Mother and the Multivocal State in 20th-Century Prince Edward Island," *Acadiensis* 38, no. 2 (2009).
30 Myers, "Apocrypha of Minnie," 8–9.
31 Myers, "Apocrypha of Minnie," 9. The similarity to Mike Hack is unmistakable.
32 Peter Gossage, "La Marâtre: Marie-Anne Houde and the Myth of the Wicked Stepmother in Quebec," *Canadian Historical Review* 76, no. 4 (1995); Matthew Nash, "The (Step)Motherly Ideal: The Role of Sex, Gender and Stereotype in the Aurore Gagnon Murder Trial," *McMaster Journal of Communication* 2, no. 1 (2005).
33 Gossage, "La Marâtre," 567.
34 Gossage, "La Marâtre," 569.
35 See Joint Committee of the Senate and House of Commons, "Final Report," Table H, p. 34. From 1920 to 1949, offenders aged 21–30 had the lowest probability of commutation.
36 Strange, "Lottery of Death," 596. Cf. Strange, "Discretionary Justice: Political Culture and the Death Penalty in New South Wales and Ontario, 1890–1920," 149–52.

# Bibliography

Abell, Jennie. "Ideology and the Emergence of Legal Aid in Saskatchewan." *Dalhousie Law Journal* 16, no. 1 (1993).
Anderson, Alan B. *Settling Saskatchewan*. Regina: University of Regina Press, 2013.
Anderson, F.W. *A Concise History of Capital Punishment in Canada*. Calgary: Frontier Publishing, 1973.
Archer, John H. *Saskatchewan: A History*. Saskatoon: Western Producer Prairie Books, 1980.
Asper, David Alan D. "Wrongful Convictions in Canada and Defence Counsel: It's Time for Mandatory Professional Education and Competency Safeguards." Masters thesis, University of Toronto, 2007.
Avio, Kenneth L. "Capital Punishment in Canada: Statistical Evidence and Constitutional Issues." *Canadian Journal of Criminology* 30, no. 4 (1988).
– "The Quality of Mercy: Exercise of the Royal Prerogative in Canada." *Canadian Public Policy* 13, no. 3 (1987).
Boudreau, Michael. "'He Was Always a Mental Defective': Psychiatric Conversations and the Execution of Bennie Swim in New Brunswick, 1922." *Journal of New Brunswick Studies* 12, no. 1 (2020).
Burton, Elaine. "The Last Hanging at the Old Port Arthur Jail: A Case Study in Capital Punishment." Course paper, University of Toronto, 1994.
Campbell, Marjorie Freeman. *A Century of Crime: The Development of Crime Detection Methods in Canada*. Toronto: McClelland & Stewart, 1970.
Chandler, David B. *Capital Punishment in Canada: A Sociological Study of Repressive Law*. Toronto: McClelland and Stewart, 1976.
Coughlan, Steve. *Criminal Procedure*, 4th ed. Toronto: Irwin Law, 2020.
Currie, Albert. "Legal Aid Delivery Models in Canada: Past Experience and Future Developments." *University of British Columbia Law Review* 33, no. 2 (2000).

Davidson, Fiona, Velimir Kovacevic, Mark Cave, Kathryn Hart, and Frances Dark. "Assessing Fitness for Trial for Deaf Defendants." *Psychiatry, Psychology and Law* 22, no. 1 (2015).

Deighton, Alex. "The Last Asylum: Experiencing the Weyburn Mental Hospital, 1921–1939." Masters thesis, University of Saskatchewan, 2016.

– "The Nature of Eugenic Thought and Limits of Eugenic Practice in Interwar Saskatchewan." In *Eugenics at the Edges of Empire: New Zealand, Australia, Canada and South Africa*, edited by Diane B. Paul, John Stenhouse, and Hamish G. Spencer, 63–84. Cham, Switzerland: Palgrave Macmillan, 2018.

Detterman, Douglas K., Lynne T. Gabriel, and Joanne M. Ruthsatz. "Intelligence and Mental Retardation." In *Handbook of Intelligence*, Robert J. Sternberg, 141–58. Cambridge: Cambridge University Press, 2000.

Dubinsky, Karen, and Franca Iacovetta. "Murder, Womanly Virtue, and Motherhood: The Case of Angelina Napolitano, 1911–1922." *Canadian Historical Review* 72, no. 4 (1991).

Dyck, Erica, and Alex Deighton. *Managing Madness: Weyburn Mental Hospital and the Transformation of Psychiatric Care in Canada*. Winnipeg: University of Manitoba Press, 2017.

Ewing, Charles Patrick. *Murder, Madness, and the Law*. Oxford: Oxford University Press, 2008.

Farrell, Ronald A., and Victoria L. Swigert. "Adjudication in Homicide: An Interpretive Analysis of the Effects of Defendant and Victim Social Characteristics." *Journal of Research in Crime and Delinquency* 23, no. 4 (1986).

Friedland, Martin L. *The Case of Valentine Shortis: A True Story of Crime and Politics in Canada*. Toronto: University of Toronto Press, 1986.

– *A Century of Criminal Justice: Perspectives on the Development of Canadian Law*. Toronto: Carswell Legal Publications, 1984.

Gadoury, Lorraine, and Antonio Lechasseur. *Persons Sentenced to Death in Canada, 1867–1976: An Inventory of Case Files in the Fonds of the Department of Justice*. Ottawa: National Archives of Canada, 1994.

Gossage, Peter. "La Marâtre: Marie-Anne Houde and the Myth of the Wicked Stepmother in Quebec." *Canadian Historical Review* 76, no. 4 (1995).

Harris, Michael. *Justice Denied: The Law Versus Donald Marshall*. Toronto: Macmillan of Canada, 1986.

Ives, Dale E. "The 'Canadian' Approach to Ineffective Assistance of Counsel Claims." *Brandeis Law Journal* 42, no. 2 (2003–4).

– "Failure to Interview a Potential Defence Witness as the Basis for an Ineffective Assistance of Counsel Claim." *Criminal Law Quarterly* 53, no. 4 (2007–8).

Joint Committee of the Senate and House of Commons. *Final Report on Capital Punishment*. Ottawa: Queen's Printer, 1956.

LeBordais, Isabel. *The Trial of Steven Truscott*. Toronto: McClelland and Stewart, 1966.

Leyton-Brown, Ken. *The Practice of Execution in Canada*. Vancouver: UBC Press, 2010.

Martin, G. Arthur. "The Role and Responsibility of the Defence Advocate." *Criminal Law Quarterly* 12, no. 4 (1970).

McCartney, Carole, and Clive Walker. "Criminal Justice and Miscarriages of Justice in England and Wales." In *Wrongful Conviction: International Perspectives on Miscarriages of Justice*, edited by C. Ronald Huff and Martin Killias. Philadelphia: Temple University Press, 2008.

McKercher, Robert B., and Bertram Wolfe. *Understanding Western Canada's Dominion Land Survey System*. Saskatoon: University of Saskatchewan, 1986.

Moran, Richard. *Knowing Right from Wrong: The Insanity Defense of Daniel M'Naghten*. New York: Free Press, 1981.

– "McNaughtan [McNaghten], Daniel." In *Oxford Dictionary of National Biography*. Oxford: Oxford University Press, 2004.

Myers, Sharon. "The Apocrypha of Minnie McGee: The Murderous Mother and the Multivocal State in 20th-Century Prince Edward Island." *Acadiensis* 38, no. 2 (2009).

Nash, Matthew. "The (Step)Motherly Ideal: The Role of Sex, Gender and Stereotype in the Aurore Gagnon Murder Trial." *McMaster Journal of Communication* 2, no. 1 (2005).

Naughton, Michael. "Redefining Miscarriages of Justice: A Revived Human-Rights Approach to Unearth Subjugated Discourses of Wrongful Criminal Conviction." *British Journal of Criminology* 45, no. 2 (2005).

– *Rethinking Miscarriages of Justice: Beyond the Tip of the Iceberg*. Houndmills: Palgrave Macmillan, 2007.

Nelligan, John P. "Legal Aid in Canada: Existing Facilities." *Canadian Bar Review* 29, no. 6 (1951).

Paciocco, David M. "A Voyage of Discovery: Examining the Precarious Condition of the Preliminary Inquiry." *Criminal Law Quarterly* 48, no. 2 (2003).

Paciocco, David M., Palma Paciocco, and Lee Struesser. *The Law of Evidence*, 8th ed. Toronto: Irwin Law, 2020.

Petersen, Myrna L. *The Pathological Casebook of Dr. Frances McGill*. Regina: Ideation Entertainment, 2005.

Petryshyn, Jaroslav, and L. Dzubak. *Peasants in the Promised Land: Canada and the Ukrainians, 1891–1914*. Toronto: James Lorimer, 1985.

Phillips, Scott. "Legal Disparities in the Capital of Capital Punishment." *Journal of Criminal Law and Criminology* 99, no. 3 (2009).

Poplak, Lorna. *Drop Dead: A Horrible History of Hanging in Canada*. Toronto: Dundurn, 2017.

Primus, Eve Brensike. "Disaggregating Ineffective Assistance of Counsel Doctrine: Four Forms of Constitutional Ineffectiveness." *Stanford Law Review* 72, no. 6 (2020).
Proulx, Michel, and David Layton. *Ethics and Canadian Criminal Law*. Toronto: Irwin Law, 2001.
Roach, Kent. *Criminal Law*, 7th ed. Toronto: Irwin Law, 2018.
– "Defining Miscarriages of Justice in the Context of Post-911 Counter-Terrorism." In *Counter-Terrorism, Constitutionalism, and Miscarriages of Justice: A Festschrift for Professor Clive Walker*, edited by Genevieve Lennon, Colin King, and Carole McCartney. Oxford: Hart Publishing, 2018.
– "Exonerating the Wrongfully Convicted: Do We Need Innocence Hearings?" In *Honouring Social Justice: Honouring Dianne Martin*, edited by Margaret E. Beare. Toronto: University of Toronto Press, 2008.
– "Wrongful Convictions in Canada." *University of Cincinnati Law Review* 80, no. 4 (2012).
– *Wrongfully Convicted: Guilty Pleas, Imagined Crimes, and What Canada Must Do to Safeguard Justice*. New York: Simon & Schuster, 2023.
Salterio, Joe L. "Fees for Defence of Indigent Persons." *Saskatchewan Bar Review and Law Society's Gazette* 14, no. 2 (1949).
Sharpe, Robert J. *The Lazier Murder: Prince Edward County, 1884*. Toronto: University of Toronto Press, 2011.
Sheehan, Thomas M. "Administrative Review and Capital Punishment: The Canadian Concept." *American Journal of Correction* 27, no. 1 (1965).
Sher, Julian. *"Until You Are Dead": Steven Truscott's Long Ride into History*. Toronto: Seal Books, 2008.
Simester, Andrew. *Fundamentals of Criminal Law: Responsibility, Culpability, and Wrongdoing*. Oxford: Oxford University Press, 2021.
Solomon, Andrew. *Far from the Tree: Parents, Children, and the Search for Identity*. New York: Scribner, 2012.
Strange, Carolyn. *The Death Penalty and Sex Murder in Canadian History*. Toronto: University of Toronto Press, 2020.
– "Discretionary Justice: Political Culture and the Death Penalty in New South Wales and Ontario, 1890–1920." In *Qualities of Mercy: Justice, Punishment, and Discretion*, edited by Carolyn Strange. Vancouver: UBC Press, 1996.
– "The Lottery of Death: Capital Punishment, 1867–1976." *Manitoba Law Journal* 23 (1995).
Sumner, Len W. *Pheasant Forks: History 1882–1905*. Toronto: Self-published, 1982.
– *Raw Prairie to Grain Elevators: The Chronicles of a Pioneer Community Duff, Saskatchewan*. Toronto: Dundurn Press, 1980.

# Bibliography

Swigert, Victoria L., and Ronald A. Farrell. "Normal Homicides and the Law." *American Sociological Review* 42, no. 1 (1977).

Tanovich, David M. "Charting the Constitutional Right of Effective Assistance of Counsel in Canada." *Criminal Law Quarterly* 36, no. 4 (1994).

– "Further Developments on Claims of Ineffectiveness of Counsel." *Criminal Reports (4th)* 34, no. 32 (1995).

Trent, James W. *Inventing the Feeble Mind: A History of Intellectual Disability in the United States*. New York: Oxford University Press, 2017.

Verdun-Jones, Simon N. "The Evolution of the Defences of Insanity and Automatism in Canada from 1843 to 1979: A Saga of Reluctance to Sever the Umbilical Cord to the Mother Country?" *University of British Columbia Law Review* 14, no. 1 (1979).

– "The Insanity Defence in Canada: Setting a New Course." *International Journal of Law and Psychiatry* 17, no. 2 (1994).

Vernon, McCay, and Katrina Miller. "Obstacles Faced by Deaf People in the Criminal Justice System." *American Annals of the Deaf* 150, no. 3 (2005).

Vernon, McCay, Annie G. Steinberg, and Louise A. Montoya. "Deaf Murderers: Clinical and Forensic Issues." *Behavioral Sciences and the Law* 17, no. 4 (1999).

Walter, Herbert J. "Rex vs. Mike Hack: Handwriting in a Murder Trial in Western Canada." *American Journal of Police Science* 3, no. 1 (1932).

Webster, Cheryl Marie. "Why Re-Open the Debate on the Preliminary Inquiry? Some Preliminary Empirical Observations." *Canadian Journal of Criminology and Criminal Justice* 55, no. 4 (2013).

White, Kimberley. *Negotiating Responsibility: Law, Murder, and States of Mind*. Vancouver and Toronto: UBC Press, 2008.

Wilson, Garrett, and Kevin Wilson. *Diefenbaker for the Defence*. Toronto: James Lorimer, 1988.

Zemans, Frederick H. "Legal Aid and Legal Advice in Canada: An Overview of the Last Decade in Quebec, Saskatchewan and Ontario." *Osgoode Hall Law Journal* 16, no. 3 (1978).

# Index

abortion, access to, 122–3
Addis, Harry, 19
Anderson, Percival McCuaig, 25–8, 38–46, 49–51, 55–7, 75–6, 91–105, 113, 115; indigent defence by, 119, 121–2; ineffective assistance of, 77–88, 104–5, 117–22
Armbruster, Phillip, 23, 72, 75, 92–3, 97
Association in Defence of the Wrongfully Convicted (AIDWYC), 29–31. *See also* Innocence Canada
Avio, Kenneth, 125–6, 128–9

Baldwin, Fred, 81–2
Baltovich, Robert, 30
Bannerman, William, 12, 14–15, 18–19, 23, 27, 34, 39, 43
Bateman, Harry, 13, 15, 23
Battersby, Luke, 13, 16, 54
Belcourt, Barney, 36, 38
Bickerdike, Robert, 48–9, 128
Blain, T.J., 73
Brensike Primus, Eve, 117, 121
Byers, Daniel Richmond, 81–2

Campbell, Alexander Douglas, 78, 84, 91, 97–100, 103–7, 116
Canadian Pacific Railway, 6
Canadian Prisoners' Welfare Association, 48, 128. *See also* National Prison Reform Association
Canora, SK, 27
Clark, Daniel, 79

Clarke, C.K., 66
clemency, application for, xi, 39, 87–9, 101, 104, 123; factors in determining outcome, 123–9. *See also* royal prerogative of mercy
cognitive impairment. *See* intellectual disability
Court of King's Bench, 26, 35–6, 38, 95, 119–20
Cromie, Thomas, 90
Crozier, James A., 82
Csada, Lyle, x
Csada, Rita, x

death penalty, 48–9, 89, 108
Diefenbaker, John George, 120–1
Diment, William, 22
Dominion Land Survey, 7
*Dominion Lands Act*, 7
Dubuc, SK, 15–16, 22–4, 46
Duff, A.E., 3
Duff, SK, ix–x, 3–6, 8–11, 13–15, 18, 22, 24; Orange Hall in, 4, 18–19, 25
Dunnett, Charles, 19

Edey, Arthur, 40–1
Edey, George, 7, 13, 15, 19, 22–4, 27–8, 40, 47, 54, 121; coroner's inquest for, 18–19; murder of, ix, 15–19, 24, 33, 38, 42–3, 46–7, 49–50, 75, 96, 125, 129
Elliott, William Stanley, 20, 25, 38, 77, 85, 87, 92, 96–7, 100–01, 117, 119
Ellis, Arthur, 82, 108–9, 111, 113

Enns, Bernard, 22
eugenics, 60, 98
evidence: circumstantial vs. forensic, 28, 39

Fairbairn, H.B., 27, 39
Findlay, C.A., 18, 27, 42–3, 45, 51
fingerprinting, 39–40
First Nations, 6–7; reserves, 7
Fritz, J., 111

Gale, William A., 27, 39
Galicia, 6, 11, 53–4
Gallagher, Michael F., 90, 94–7, 100, 102–6, 116, 124, 126
Galton, Francis, 60
Geddes, A.L., 96–7, 100, 104
Gerrand, Ernest Walter, 25, 27, 38
Goddard, Henry Herbert, 60
Goldsmith, T.C., 25
Gottinger, Fred, 23
Gottinger, Louie, 19
grand jury, 24
Grand Trunk Pacific Railway, 3, 35
Great Depression, 4
Gross, Pete, 15

Hack, Dorothea (Ulmer), 11, 20, 22–3, 45, 49, 54, 69–72, 74–5, 92, 97
Hack, Dorothy (Hepting), x, 16, 20, 22–4, 47, 74, 111
Hack, Elizabeth (Mayer), x
Hack, Frederick, 22, 69–74, 80, 92, 97
Hack, Katie (Schick), 71
Hack, Mathias, 11, 20, 54, 69, 71, 74
Hack, Mathias, Jr., 22
Hack, Michael (Mike), 11, 14, 22–4, 38, 47, 54–6, 91, 116; application for clemency, ix, 89–107; charge (murder), ix, 19; charge (theft), 54, 73, 91; deafness of, 15, 26, 34, 39, 56, 73, 83–4, 126, 129; ethnicity of, 51–5, 126, 129; execution of, ix, 93, 109–14; grave of, 114–15; intellectual disability of, 69–70, 74–5, 84–5, 106, 126, 129; interrogation of, 15–16; investigation of, 18–19; miscarriage of justice for, 34, 50–68, 86–8, 104; poverty of, 122–3, 129;
preliminary inquiry for, 19, 24–8; sentence of (murder), 49; sentence of (theft), 73; temperament of, 70–2; trial of (murder), ix, 28, 35–49; trial of (theft), 73, 91; wrongful conviction of, 33–4, 50–68, 86–7
Haverstock, Fred, 15
Hayes, Tom, 109, 112
Hays, Charles Melville, 25
Hepting, George, 16, 20, 22–4, 47, 111
Houde, Anne-Marie, 128

identity: horizontal, 74; vertical, 70–4
indigent defence systems, 117–21; private bar vs. staff lawyer, 118
ineffective assistance of counsel, xi, 76–7, 117–18; episodic vs. pervasive, 117; personal vs. structural, 117
Innocence Canada, 30. *See also* Association in Defence of the Wrongfully Convicted
insanity, defence of, xi, 37–68, 79–82, 105
intellectual disability, 60–1; Binet–Simon IQ tests for, 60, 78; degrees of, 60; imbecility, 60–1, 78, 106

Johnson, Arthur, 14–15, 23
Johnston, Charles J., 82
Justice, Department of, 39

Kaduhr, Herman, 15
Kaufman, Fred, 31
Keown, Bert, 119–20
King, W.W., 73
Krahn, Walter, 69, 71–2, 92–3, 97

Laight, J., 27, 44
Lapointe, Ernest, 91, 94–5, 100, 103–5, 116, 124, 126
Lazier, Peter, 52
LeBordais, Isabel, 30
Lee, Michael, 79–80
Lemberg, SK, 6, 11, 18, 51, 54, 72
Lewis, J. Grant, 18
Lorlie, SK, 15–16, 28, 41–2, 75
Lowder, David, 52
Lowder, George, 52

# Index

Lutz, Louis, 22–3
Lutz, Matthew, 22

Maclean, Donald, 37, 42–3, 45–51, 78–80, 84, 86, 93–7, 100–3, 116, 125–6; charge to the jury, 46–51
MacNeill, James Walter, 97, 100, 104–7, 116, 119–20
Malloy, Anne, 64–5
Mann, Joseph, 23
Marshall, Donald, Jr., 30, 33
Martin, G. Arthur, 87
Marwood, William, 108
Mathieu, Michel, 66
Matthews, John W.: as coroner, x, 17–18; as justice of the peace, x, 19, 25, 27–8
Matthews, Tom, 13–15, 17, 74
Matthews, Sid, 74
McGee, Minnie, 127
McGill, Frances, 18
McGill, William, 112
McIntosh, Linden Y., 82
McKay, James, 35
Melfort, SK, 119
Melville, SK, x, 3, 5, 7, 12, 15, 19, 25, 35, 124; city hall, 35–6; Judicial District of, 25, 35
Melville *Advance*, 52
mental disorder, defence of. *See* insanity, defence of
Metcalfe, J.G., 19, 54, 56, 91
Metcalfe, W.G., 79
Middleton, Andrew, 22–3
Milgaard, David, 30
Minassian, Alek, 64–5
miscarriage of justice, xi, 34
M'Naghten, Daniel, 57–60, 64, 67–8
M'Naghten Rules, 58–61, 65–6
Morin, Guy Paul, 29–31, 33–4, 85, 88
murder: capital and non-capital, 49; definition of, 46
Mulock, William, 66
Mulvey, Thomas, 93–4

Napolitano, Angelina, 123–5
National Prison Reform Association, 48. *See also* Canadian Prisoners' Welfare Association

Neudorf, SK, 6, 11, 15, 20, 23–4, 27, 39, 51, 54, 69, 73, 96
Niebergall, Jacob, 71, 92–3, 97

Olson, Ernest, 119–21

Pasowesty, John, 120–1
Pheasant Forks, 10
Pheasant Hills, x, 6–7, 10, 51, 68, 70, 77, 79; ethnic composition of, 51–2
Phillion, Romeo, 30, 32
preliminary inquiry, 24–5
Primitive Methodist Colonization Company, x, 10, 51
Prince Albert, SK, 120
psychopathy, 106–7

*R. v. Morgentaler*, 122
Regina, SK, 3, 7, 12, 19, 25, 77, 119, 124
Regina Cemetery, ix, 115
Regina Jail, ix, 19, 28, 49, 73, 78, 97, 100, 105, 109–11; scaffold in, 110–11
Remission Service, 90, 93–5, 101–3, 126
Rhéaume, Bernard, 55
Riel, Louis, 48
Roach, Kent, 126
Rothwell, Oswald E., 78, 100, 103–6, 113
Royal Canadian Mounted Police (RCMP), 12, 19, 40, 90
royal prerogative of mercy, xi, 89–90. *See also* clemency, application for
Royal Proclamation of 1763, 6

Sampson, Herbert E., 38, 45, 49, 75, 84, 100, 103, 116, 120, 126
Sarao, Tomasina, 109
Saskatchewan, province of, 6–7, 12, 98–9; homesteading in, 7–10; indigent defence system of, 118–19
Saskatchewan Court of Appeal, 26, 38, 67, 86, 119
Saskatchewan Law Society, 118
Saskatchewan Mental Hospital, 68, 97
Saskatchewan Penitentiary, 109
Saskatchewan Provincial Police (SPP), 12, 19, 25, 27, 40
Saskatoon, SK, 124
Schick, Jacob, 71

Schick, Louie, 15
Scott, W.B., 19
Shortis, Valentine, 65–6, 80
Slater, J.G., 73
Small, Lennie, 75
Solomon, Andrew, 70, 73
Sophonow, Thomas, 30
Squires, Frederick Charles, 81
Stephen, James Fitzjames, 59, 62
Strange, Carolyn, 87, 129
Sumner, Frank, x
Sumner, Len W., ix–xi
Supreme Court (Canada), 25, 61–4, 76
Supreme Court (United States), 76
Sutton, Edmund, 19, 22–4
Swim, Bennie, 81

Taylor, George E., 120
Thomset, Joseph, 52
Towns, Harry, 41–2
Truscott, Stephen, 30–3, 88
Tyrer, Thomas George, 27, 39

Ulmer, Sam, 23
Ulmer, Willie, 23
unfitness to stand trial, xi, 67, 82–5

Walter, Herbert J., 44–5
*War Measures Act*, 53–4; internment of Ukrainians, 53–4
Ward, May, 22
Ward, Reginald, 13, 18, 22–3
Watts, James, 12, 16, 18–20, 27, 34, 43
Wetzstein, C.T., 101, 109, 112–13, 115
Weyburn Mental Hospital, 68, 78, 91, 98–9
Wilkinson, Martin., 101, 109, 113
wrongful conviction, xi, 29–34; and factual innocence, 30–4, 50; external standard of, 32–3; internal standard of, 33. *See also* miscarriage of justice
Wynyard, SK, 120

Yorkton, SK, 124

PUBLICATIONS OF THE OSGOODE SOCIETY FOR CANADIAN LEGAL HISTORY

2024  Adam Dodek, *Heenan Blaikie: The Making and Unmaking of a Great Canadian Law Firm*
Colin Campbell and Robert Raizenne, *A History of Canadian Income Tax Volume II, 1948–71*
Wayne Sumner, *Prairie Justice: The Hanging of Mike Hack*
Ian Radforth, *Deadly Swindle: An 1890 Murder in Backwoods Ontario That Gripped the World*

2023  Lori Chambers and Joan Sangster, eds., *Essays in the History of Canadian Law Volume XII: New Perspectives on Gender and the Law*
Ian Kyer, *The Ontario Bond Scandal of 1924 Re-examined*
Jonathan Swainger, *The Notorious Georges: Crime and Community in British Columbia's Northern Interior, 1909–25*

2022  Jim Phillips, Philip Girard, and R. Blake Brown, *A History of Law in Canada Volume II: Law for the New Dominion, 1867–1914*
J. Barry Wright, Susan Binnie, and Eric Tucker, eds., *Canadian State Trials Volume V: World War, Cold War and Challenges to Sovereignty, 1939–1990*
Constance Backhouse, *Reckoning with Racism: Police, Judges and the RDS Case*

2021  Daniel Rûck *The Laws and the Land: The Settler Colonial Invasion of Kahnawà:ke in Nineteenth-Century Canada*
Lyndsay Campbell, *Truth and Privilege: Libel Law in Massachusetts and Nova Scotia, 1820–1840*
Martine Valois, Ian Greene, Craig Forcese, and Peter McCormick, eds. *The Federal Court of Appeal and the Federal Court: Fifty Years of History*
Colin Campbell and Robert Raizenne, *A History of Canadian Income Tax Volume I: The Income War Tax Act 1917–1948*

2020  Heidi Bohaker, *Doodem and Council Fire: Anishinaabe Governance through Alliance*
Carolyn Strange, *The Death Penalty and Sex Murder in Canadian History*

2019  Harry Arthurs, *Connecting the Dots: The Life of an Academic Lawyer*
Eric Reiter, *Wounded Feelings: Litigating Emotions in Quebec, 1870–1950*

2018  Philip Girard, Jim Phillips, and Blake Brown, *A History of Law in Canada Volume 1: Beginnings to 1866*
Suzanne Chiodo, *The Class Actions Controversy: The Origins and Development of the Ontario Class Proceedings Act*

2017  Constance Backhouse, *Claire L'Heureux-Dube: A Life*
Dennis G. Molinaro, *An Exceptional Law: Section 98 and the Emergency State, 1919–1936*

2016  Lori Chambers, *A Legal History of Adoption in Ontario, 1921–2015*
Bradley Miller, *Boarderline Crime: Fugitive Criminals and the Challenge of the Boarder, 1819–1914*
James Muir, *Law, Debt, and Merchant Power: The Civil Courts of Eighteenth-Century Halifax*

2015 Barry Wright, Eric Tucker, and Susan Binnie, eds., *Canadian State Trails Volume IV: Security, Dissent and the Limits of Toleration in War and Peace, 1914–1939*
David Fraser, *"Honorary Protestants": The Jewish School Question in Montreal, 1867–1997*
C. Ian Kyer, *A Thirty Years' War: The Failed Public /Private Partnership that Spurred the Creation of The Toronto Transit Commission, 1891–1921*

2014 Christopher Moore, *The Court of Appeal for Ontario: Defining the Right of Appeal, 1792–2013*
Dominique Clément, *Equality Deferred: Sex Discrimination and British Columbia's Human Rights State, 1953–84*
Paul Craven, *Petty Justice: Low Law and the Sessions System in Charlotte County, New Brunswick, 1785–1867*
Thomas Telfer, *Ruin and Redemption: The Struggle for a Canadian Bankruptcy Law, 1867–1919*

2013 Roy McMurtry, *Memoirs and Reflections*
Charlotte Gray, *The Massey Murder: A Maid, Her Master and the Trial That Shocked a Nation*
C. Ian Kyer, *Lawyers, Families, and Businesses: The Shaping of a Bay Street Law Firm, Faskens 1863–1963*
G. Blaine Baker and Donald Fyson, eds., *Essays in the History of Canadian Law Volume 11: Quebec and the Canadas*

2012 R. Blake Brown, *Arming and Disarming: A History of Gun Control in Canada*
Eric Tucker, James Muir, and Bruce Ziff, eds., *Property on Trial: Canadian Cases in Context*
Shelley A.M. Gavigan, *Hunger, Horses, and Government Men: Criminal Law on the Aboriginal Plains, 1870–1905*
Barrington Walker, ed., *The African Canadian Legal Odyssey: Historical Essays*

2011 Robert J. Sharpe, *The Lazier Murder: Prince Edward County, 1884*
Philip Girard, *Lawyers and Legal Culture in British North America: Beamish Murdoch of Halifax*
John McLaren, *Dewigged, Bothered, and Bewildered: British Colonial Judges on Trial*
Lesley Erickson, *Westward Bound: Sex, Violence, the Law, and the Making of a Settler Society*

2010 Judy Fudge and Eric Tucker, eds., *Work on Trial: Canadian Labour Law Struggles*
Christopher Moore, *The British Columbia Court of Appeal: The First Hundred Years*
Frederick Vaughan, *Viscount Haldane: The Wicked Step-father of the Canadian Constitution*
Barrington Walker, *Race on Trial: Black Defendants in Ontario's Criminal Courts, 1850–1950*

2009   William Kaplan, *Canadian Maverick: The Life and Times of Ivan C. Rand*
       R. Blake Brown, *A Trying Question: The Jury in Nineteenth-Century Canada*
       Barry Wright and Susan Binnie, eds., *Canadian State Trials Volume 3: Political Trials and Security Measures, 1840–1914*
       Robert J. Sharpe, *The Last Day, the Last Hour: The Currie Libel Trial*
2008   Constance Backhouse, *Carnal Crimes: Sexual Assault Law in Canada, 1900–1975*
       Jim Phillips, R. Roy McMurtry, and John Saywell, eds., *Essays in the History of Canadian Law. Volume 10: A Tribute to Peter N. Oliver*
       Gregory Taylor, *The Law of the Land: Canada's Receptions of the Torrens System*
       Hamar Foster, Benjamin Berger, and A.R. Buck, eds., *The Grand Experiment: Law and Legal Culture in British Settler Societies*
2007   Robert Sharpe and Patricia McMahon, *The Persons Case: The Origins and Legacy of the Fight for Legal Personhood*
       Lori Chambers, *Misconceptions: Unmarried Motherhood and the Ontario Children of Unmarried Parents Act, 1921–1969*
       Jonathan Swainger, ed., *The Alberta Supreme Court at 100: History and Authority*
       Martin Friedland, *My Life in Crime and Other Academic Adventures*
2006   Donald Fyson, *Magistrates, Police and People: Everyday Criminal Justice in Quebec and Lower Canada, 1764–1837*
       Dale Brawn, *The Court of Queen's Bench of Manitoba 1870–1950: A Biographical History*
       R.C.B. Risk, *A History of Canadian Legal Thought: Collected Essays*, edited and introduced by G. Blaine Baker and Jim Phillips
2005   Philip Girard, *Bora Laskin: Bringing Law to Life*
       Christopher English, ed., *Essays in the History of Canadian Law Volume 9: Two Islands, Newfoundland and Prince Edward Island*
       Fred Kaufman, *Searching for Justice: An Autobiography*
2004   John D. Honsberger, *Osgoode Hall: An Illustrated History*
       Frederick Vaughan, *Aggressive in Pursuit: The Life of Justice Emmett Hall*
       Constance Backhouse and Nancy Backhouse, *The Heiress versus the Establishment: Mrs. Campbell's Campaign for Legal Justice*
       Philip Girard, Jim Phillips, and Barry Cahill, eds., *The Supreme Court of Nova Scotia, 1754–2004: From Imperial Bastion to Provincial Oracle*
2003   Robert Sharpe and Kent Roach, *Brian Dickson: A Judge's Journey*
       George Finlayson, *John J. Robinette: Peerless Mentor*
       Peter Oliver, *The Conventional Man: The Diaries of Ontario Chief Justice Robert A. Harrison, 1856–1878*
       Jerry Bannister, *The Rule of the Admirals: Law, Custom and Naval Government in Newfoundland, 1699–1832*

2002   John T. Saywell, *The Law Makers: Judicial Power and the Shaping of Canadian Federalism*
       David Murray, *Colonial Justice: Justice, Morality and Crime in the Niagara District, 1791–1849*
       F. Murray Greenwood and Barry Wright, eds., *Canadian State Trials Volume 2: Rebellion and Invasion in the Canadas, 1837–1839*
       Patrick Brode, *Courted and Abandoned: Seduction in Canadian Law*
2001   Ellen Anderson, *Judging Bertha Wilson: Law as Large as Life*
       Judy Fudge and Eric Tucker, *Labour before the Law: Collective Action in Canada, 1900–1948*
       Laurel Sefton MacDowell, *Renegade Lawyer: The Life of J.L. Cohen*
2000   Barry Cahill, *"The Thousandth Man": A Biography of James McGregor Stewart*
       A.B. McKillop, *The Spinster and the Prophet: Florence Deeks, H.G. Wells, and the Mystery of the Purloined Past*
       Beverley Boissery and F. Murray Greenwood, *Uncertain Justice: Canadian Women and Capital Punishment*
       Bruce Ziff, *Unforeseen Legacies: Reuben Wells Leonard and the Leonard Foundation Trust*
1999   Constance Backhouse, *Colour-Coded: A Legal History of Racism in Canada, 1900–1950*
       G. Blaine Baker and Jim Phillips, eds., *Essays in the History of Canadian Law Volume 8: In Honour of R.C.B. Risk*
       Richard W. Pound, *Chief Justice W.R. Jackett: By the Law of the Land*
       David Vanek, *Fulfilment: Memoirs of a Criminal Court Judge*
1998   Sidney Harring, *White Man's Law: Native People in Nineteenth-Century Canadian Jurisprudence*
       Peter Oliver, *"Terror to Evil-Doers": Prisons and Punishments in Nineteenth-Century Ontario*
1997   James W. St. G. Walker, *"Race," Rights and the Law in the Supreme Court of Canada: Historical Case Studies*
       Lori Chambers, *Married Women and Property Law in Victorian Ontario*
       Patrick Brode, *Casual Slaughters and Accidental Judgments: Canadian War Crimes and Prosecutions, 1944–1948*
       Ian Bushnell, *The Federal Court of Canada: A History, 1875–1992*
1996   Carol Wilton, ed., *Essays in the History of Canadian Law Volume 7: Inside the Law – Canadian Law Firms in Historical Perspective*
       William Kaplan, *Bad Judgment: The Case of Mr. Justice Leo A. Landreville*
       Murray Greenwood and Barry Wright, eds., *Canadian State Trials Volume 1: Law, Politics and Security Measures, 1608–1837*
1995   David Williams, *Just Lawyers: Seven Portraits*
       Hamar Foster and John McLaren, eds., *Essays in the History of Canadian Law Volume 6: British Columbia and the Yukon*
       W.H. Morrow, ed., *Northern Justice: The Memoirs of Mr. Justice William G. Morrow*
       Beverley Boissery, *A Deep Sense of Wrong: The Treason, Trials and Transportation to New South Wales of Lower Canadian Rebels after the 1838 Rebellion*

1994 Patrick Boyer, *A Passion for Justice: The Legacy of James Chalmers McRuer*
Charles Pullen, *The Life and Times of Arthur Maloney: The Last of the Tribunes*
Jim Phillips, Tina Loo, and Susan Lewthwaite, eds., *Essays in the History of Canadian Law Volume 5: Crime and Criminal Justice*
Brian Young, *The Politics of Codification: The Lower Canadian Civil Code of 1866*
1993 Greg Marquis, *Policing Canada's Century: A History of the Canadian Association of Chiefs of Police*
Murray Greenwood, *Legacies of Fear: Law and Politics in Quebec in the Era of the French Revolution*
1992 Brendan O'Brien, *Speedy Justice: The Tragic Last Voyage of His Majesty's Vessel* Speedy
Robert Fraser, ed., *Provincial Justice: Upper Canadian Legal Portraits from the Dictionary of Canadian Biography*
1991 Constance Backhouse, *Petticoats and Prejudice: Women and Law in Nineteenth-Century Canada*
1990 Philip Girard and Jim Phillips, eds., *Essays in the History of Canadian Law Volume 3: Nova Scotia*
Carol Wilton, ed., *Essays in the History of Canadian Law Volume 4: Beyond the Law – Lawyers and Business in Canada 1830–1930*
1989 Desmond Brown, *The Genesis of the Canadian Criminal Code of 1892*
Patrick Brode, *The Odyssey of John Anderson*
1988 Robert Sharpe, *The Last Day, the Last Hour: The Currie Libel Trial*
John D. Arnup, *Middleton: The Beloved Judge*
1987 C. Ian Kyer and Jerome Bickenbach, *The Fiercest Debate: Cecil A. Wright, the Benchers and Legal Education in Ontario, 1923–1957*
1986 Paul Romney, *Mr. Attorney: The Attorney General for Ontario in Court, Cabinet and Legislature, 1791–1899*
Martin Friedland, *The Case of Valentine Shortis: A True Story of Crime and Politics in Canada*
1985 James Snell and Frederick Vaughan, *The Supreme Court of Canada: History of the Institution*
1984 Patrick Brode, *Sir John Beverley Robinson: Bone and Sinew of the Compact*
David Williams, *Duff: A Life in the Law*
1983 David H. Flaherty, ed., *Essays in the History of Canadian Law Volume 2*
1982 Marion MacRae and Anthony Adamson, *Cornerstones of Order: Courthouses and Town Halls of Ontario, 1784–1914*
1981 David H. Flaherty, ed., *Essays in the History of Canadian Law Volume 1*